THE WEIGHT OF NOTHING

Reflections from Above

Book III of *The Weight Trilogy*

by
Chetan Rao

On the M.A.R.C. Publishers
(www.onthemarcpub.com)

Copyright Page

The Weight of Nothing: Reflections from Above

First Edition

This is a work of fiction. Names, characters, places, and events are products of the author's imagination or are used fictitiously. Any resemblance to actual persons, living or dead, is purely coincidental.

Published by **On the M.A.R.C. Publishers**

www.onthemarcpub.com

ISBN (Paperback): 979-8-9936911-9-0

Cover design by On the M.A.R.C. Publishers

Printed in the United States of America

Dedication

For those who ask questions that may never have final answers, and for those who continue asking them anyway.

Foreword

A Different Vantage

A single life can be understood from many vantage points. Each reveals a different truth.

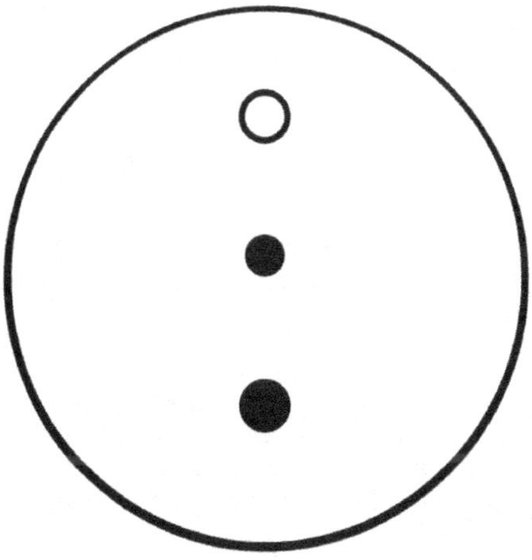

This book completes a journey that began with the first volume of The Weight Trilogy.

Each of the three books observes the same human life from a different vantage point.

The first volume, *The Weight of Shadows: Reflections from the Edge*, explores the experience of living from within the intensity of human struggle. It observes the pressures that shape a life—ambition, responsibility, loss, doubt—and the ways individuals attempt to carry those burdens while continuing forward. It is a book about the weight of experience itself.

The second volume, *The Weight of Grace: Reflections from the Center*, moves toward balance. It examines the quiet moments in which individuals begin to observe their lives rather than simply react to them. In that space, the possibility of presence appears. Life continues with all its demands, but a different relationship with those demands begins to emerge.

The third volume, *The Weight of Nothing: Reflections from Above*, takes one step further.

It explores the perspective that appears when the boundaries through which human life is normally experienced—identity, time, and separation—begin to dissolve.

Throughout history, both scientific inquiry and spiritual traditions have suggested that the individual mind may not be the final boundary of awareness. Philosophers have long considered the possibility that the observer and the observed are not entirely separate. Modern explorations of consciousness have raised similar questions in different languages.

This book approaches those ideas not as theory, but as narrative.

The voice that speaks in these pages is not confined to a single life. It observes events from the vantage that appears when human identity no longer defines the limits of awareness.

From that perspective, the story of a life does not end when the body ceases to function.

Influence continues.

Ideas propagate through other minds.

Questions move across generations.

Lives intersect in ways that gradually reveal larger patterns.

Human beings often search for meaning within the boundaries of their individual experiences.

Yet when those boundaries soften, another understanding begins to emerge.

Life is not a sequence of isolated stories.

It is a network of relationships through which awareness gradually comes to recognize itself.

The three books in this trilogy trace that movement.

From the weight of experience, to the balance of presence, to the realization that, from a wider vantage, the burdens we carry may not belong entirely to us at all.

Perhaps the observer and the observed were never separate.

Perhaps a life is simply one vantage point from which the universe briefly learns to see itself.

Principal Figures

Sharan

Engineer, writer, teacher, and father. His reflections form the foundation of the narrative that unfolds across the trilogy.

Karma

Sharan's mother. Her quiet strength, spiritual steadiness, and unconditional love make her the unseen foundation of the family's life across generations.

Sunita

Physician and medical educator. Sharan's wife and a central stabilizing presence within the family.

Karan

Engineer, businessman, and researcher whose life journey carries many of the questions explored across the three books.

Diana

Scientist and Karan's partner. Her presence introduces balance and intellectual companionship within the unfolding narrative.

Sarla

Sharan and Sunita's daughter. A physician whose life in Sangli reflects the continuity of family and service.

Naveen

Sarla's husband and medical practitioner.

Adi

The youngest generation in the family, whose childhood observations quietly echo the curiosity that runs through earlier generations.

Prologue

What we call a life may only be a moment when awareness gathers itself and looks outward.

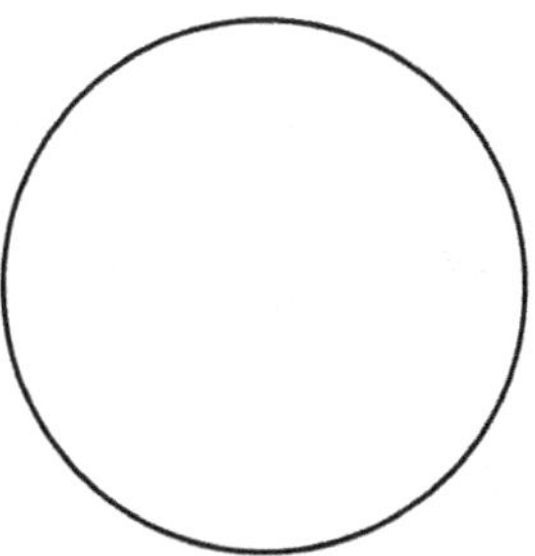

Every life appears complete when seen from within its own boundaries.

We wake, grow, struggle, love, and eventually disappear, leaving behind memories that slowly soften with time. From the inside, these events feel central and definitive. Each decision seems to shape the future in ways that matter deeply to the person making it.

Yet when observed from a wider vantage, a life begins to resemble something different.

Not an isolated story.

A temporary point of observation.

For a brief period, awareness gathers itself within a single body and looks outward through the narrow lens of identity. It experiences the world through senses, relationships, responsibilities, and questions that seem uniquely personal.

But the patterns that shape those experiences rarely begin with the individual.

They arise from histories already in motion.

Families.

Ideas.

Cultures.

Questions that have traveled quietly through generations.

A single life does not originate these currents.

It joins them.

And eventually it releases them again.

The reflections that follow observe such a life from a different perspective.

Not from within the boundaries of the person who lived it, but from the wider field in which that life briefly appeared.

From there, events that once seemed separate reveal connections.

Influence becomes visible across time.

And the questions that moved through one mind can be seen continuing their journey through many others.

From that perspective, a life is not a closed narrative.

It is a momentary window through which the universe briefly observes itself.

CHAPTER 1
A Boy Learns Silence

Silence is not emptiness. It is the place where attention begins.

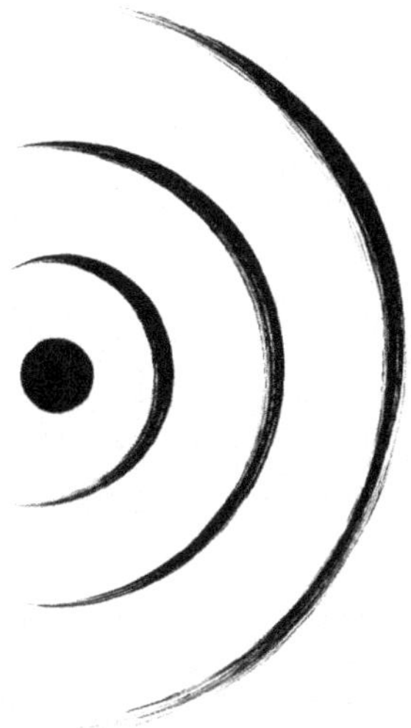

Belgaum, India, 1940.

I was born into a country that did not yet belong to itself.

I did not know that sentence then. I did not have the words for country, or rule, or belonging. I had other words. Stone. Milk. Heat. Hunger. Sleep. I had the language of a child, which is mostly body and instinct, and the small private measurements of safety.

The first thing I remember clearly is not a face. It is the floor.

Cold under my feet in the early morning, before the sun climbed high enough to warm the courtyard. The floor was always the same—hard, dependable, indifferent. When I was older, I would learn that most of life was like that. It does not soften because you are small. It softens only when someone else decides to soften it for you.

In our house, softness came from my mother.

But the house itself—our house—was not built for softness. It was built for continuity.

A joint family is not a single home. It is a moving organism. It is a set of agreements made long before you are born, and expectations that arrive with your name. There are bodies in every room, voices in every hallway, hands always reaching for something—water, cloth, money, reassurance, salt, fire.

My father's generation alone had seven brothers and one sister. Seven. When I say it now it sounds exaggerated, like a story told for effect, but it was simply our reality: seven men with seven sets of wants, seven sets of pride, seven sets of fatigue. Add their wives, add children, add the elders who sat like quiet pillars at the center of everything, and you understand why the house was never truly silent.

If you wanted solitude, you found it in small places: behind the water pots, near the back door where the light was weak, in the few minutes before dawn when even arguments were asleep.

My father, Sanad, was the oldest.

That one detail shaped the entire architecture of our life.

In India, the eldest son is not merely a son. He is a caretaker by default. He becomes the hinge the door swings on. He becomes the roof beam. He becomes the person everyone calls when something breaks, even if he did not break it.

Sanad did not ask for that role. He inherited it like land.

And yet, he was not the kind of man who walked around with duty stitched to his face. My father liked to have fun. He liked a crowded room, loud stories, music played a little too late. He liked being admired. He liked the lift in people's expressions when he entered. He could take a heavy day and make it lighter for a moment, and when you live in a world that is heavy by default, that kind of talent is not nothing.

Still, fun does not keep a household upright.

When the rice ran low. When someone's fever would not break. When a quarrel between brothers grew sharp enough to cut, it was not my father who people turned toward. It was my mother, Karma.

Karma was the salt of the earth, which is a phrase people use when they do not want to romanticize a person but still want to honor them. My mother was not sentimental. She did not speak in long speeches. She did not decorate hardship with philosophy.

She worked.

She woke before dawn, her bangles making a soft sound as she moved through the dark. She checked the water first—always the water. Then the stove. Then the grain. Then the children. Then the elders. The sequence never changed. It was as if she believed the house would collapse if her order collapsed.

Food appeared because she made it appear. Shirts were clean because she washed them. When someone was sick, she became a quiet nurse. When someone was angry, she became a quiet boundary. She did not win arguments. She simply prevented them from becoming disasters.

She was a caretaker the way the earth is a caretaker: steady, silent, unthanked, essential.

Above my parents was my grandfather, Pawan.

Pawan was a schoolteacher, a theologian, and a successful business person in insurance—three identities that, on paper, do not belong to the same man. But in him they did.

He taught children during the day. He read and discussed scripture in the evenings. And in between, he built a practical business that—strangely—fit his theology perfectly. Insurance, he said, was not about money. It was about dignity.

"When the roof breaks," I once heard him tell a neighbor who had come to argue about a policy, "the poor should not also break."

He spoke calmly. No anger. No performance. The neighbor arrived with heat and left with quiet.

I was too young to understand the mechanics of insurance. But I understood what my grandfather valued. He valued preparation. He valued steadiness. He valued the kind of faith that did not rely on miracles.

He was respected in our community in a way that was different from fear. People did not avoid him; they sought him. They asked him to arbitrate disputes. They asked him to read a situation the way he read books—slowly, precisely, without panic.

In the evenings, he sometimes sat with papers spread out on a low table. Student notebooks. Ledgers. Receipts. Pages of scripture with thin margins and dense print. He moved between them as if each was simply another form of education.

I watched him the way children watch adults when they are trying to learn what adulthood is.

We children were four: my brother, my two sisters, and me. We moved in a cluster, like small birds. We fought over nothing. We made alliances that lasted for hours and then broke them. We learned to share space, which is another way of saying we learned to shrink ourselves.

A joint family teaches you early that attention is not something you own.

It is something that passes over you like sunlight. Sometimes it warms you. Sometimes it moves on before you are ready.

At night, we slept close. In the hot months, bodies were sticky and restless. In the cooler months, we curled into each other as if warmth was a resource that might run out. The house had its own sounds at night: an uncle clearing his throat, a baby crying, a distant dog barking, the soft drag of my mother's slippers as she checked on everyone one last time.

That was where I learned silence.

Not the silence of emptiness, but the silence of listening.

The kind of silence that notices. The kind of silence that remembers.

Outside the home, India was changing in a way that even a child could feel.

I didn't understand the British. I didn't understand what it meant to be ruled. But I understood restraint. I understood caution.

I saw it in the way men's voices dropped when a stranger walked by. In the way adults interrupted themselves mid-sentence. In the way my father's laughter sometimes ended too suddenly, as if he had remembered that joy had limits.

In Belgaum, as in most towns, history arrived through small channels: newspapers passed hand to hand, radio broadcasts that made adults gather close, visitors who came from other places carrying news like baggage.

Some evenings, men gathered in our courtyard. They sat on woven charpoys and low stools. Someone would light a beedi. Someone would mention a name and the room would tilt.

Gandhi. Nehru. Congress. Freedom.

I heard those words before I understood them. I heard them the way a child hears the name of a storm forming far away. You can't see it yet, but the adults change their posture. They look toward the horizon more often.

My grandfather listened carefully. He asked questions. He weighed answers.

My father, Sanad, liked to keep the air light. He poured tea. He told stories. He tried to turn worry into laughter, as if laughter could make a problem smaller.

My mother stayed near the doorway, half-present, as women often were—hearing everything, acknowledging little.

It is strange what a boy learns by watching women. You learn what is real. You learn what matters. You learn what men perform and what women repair.

On the morning of August 15, 1947, I did not wake up thinking the world had changed.

I woke up because the house woke up. I was a little over seven years old.

There was a busyness that felt different—more charged, more alert. Voices carried a brightness that I couldn't name. Someone had come early with news, and the news moved through the house like wind.

India was free.

That is what the adults said. I did not comprehend.

Free.

The word sounded like a door opening.

I remember my father stepping into the courtyard, adjusting his shirt, his hair oiled and combed neatly as if the day required dignity. I remember my mother's hands moving faster than usual, preparing tea, preparing food, preparing the house to receive visitors who would surely arrive. I remember my grandfather sitting still for longer than normal, as if he wanted to feel the moment fully before he spoke.

Later, someone turned on the radio. The sound crackled. Adults leaned in. The voice from the radio carried a weight that made even children quiet.

I did not understand the speech. I understood what it did to people.

Some of the men smiled as if they had been holding their breath for years. Some looked uneasy, as if freedom was not only a gift but also a test.

When the broadcast ended, there was noise—talking, laughing, arguing. And then, surprisingly, there was a pause. A hush that lasted only a few seconds, but in those seconds I could feel something settle in the room.

My grandfather stood and lit a lamp.

It was not dramatic. He did not announce it. He simply placed the lamp carefully in front of a framed image and lit the wick. The flame caught, trembled once, then steadied.

"Freedom," he said quietly, not to the room but into the room, "is not the end of struggle."

Someone laughed, not mockingly, but nervously, as if the sentence was too heavy for a day that was supposed to be light.

My grandfather looked at him gently. "It is the beginning of responsibility," he added.

In that moment, I didn't understand his words. But I understood his tone.

He was not trying to dampen celebration. He was trying to prepare people for reality.

Outside our house, the town had changed its face. People walked with more purpose. Flags appeared in places that had never shown flags before. Men greeted each other with more heat, more certainty. There was singing somewhere. There were drums. Someone shouted something about the future.

But there were also whispers.

Partition.

I did not know what partition meant. I knew it made adults quieter.

In the following days, joy and fear began to travel together, like two men walking side by side who did not trust each other but could not separate. Stories arrived faster than facts. Trains filled with people. Families leaving homes. Violence in places far away, and then not so far away.

I remember seeing my mother pause once, mid-motion, holding a steel cup, listening to a neighbor speak urgently at the door. My mother's face did not change dramatically, but her eyes did. The eyes are where fear hides when the mouth refuses to confess it.

My father tried to keep the house buoyant. "Don't listen to every rumor," he said often. "We will be fine." He believed in optimism the way some men believe in prayer.

My grandfather believed in preparation.

That week, he sat me down with a small page and asked me to read.

I was still learning. I could recognize some letters, some words. I stumbled. I guessed. I watched his face for approval.

"Slowly," he said. "Don't rush. Rushing is how people misunderstand."

Then he tapped the page with a finger.

"Read what is written," he said. "And also what is not."

I looked at him, confused. "How do you read what is not written?" I asked.

He smiled a little, as if he had been waiting for the question.

"You watch," he said. "You listen. You notice what people avoid. You notice what makes them speak faster. You notice what makes them silent."

That was the first time someone explained silence to me as a tool.

In the months that followed, I practiced without knowing I was practicing.

I watched my father, Sanad, manage the joint family's obligations with varying success. I watched him play the role of caretaker because it was his role, even when his personality wanted something else. I watched him soothe disputes with jokes, sometimes effectively, sometimes not.

I watched my mother do the invisible work that kept everything from collapsing. She absorbed the overflow. She adjusted meals when money tightened. She stretched lentils, stretched patience, stretched herself. When someone criticized her, she didn't argue; she simply continued. There are forms of strength that don't look like strength until you try to live without them.

I watched my grandfather, Pawan, become an anchor for more than our family. People came to him for advice. They asked him what was safe, what was true, what was rumor, what was panic. He did not pretend to know everything. He told people what he knew and admitted what he didn't.

"A free country," I heard him tell a man one evening, "is like a free man. He must decide what kind of person he will be."

That sentence appeared again and again in different forms, like a refrain. My grandfather liked ideas that could be applied at many levels—nation, family, person.

One afternoon, I followed him through the neighborhood. He walked slowly, greeting people with a nod, stopping when someone called out. A shopkeeper asked him whether business would collapse. A neighbor asked him whether riots would reach us. An anxious young man asked him if it was time to leave.

My grandfather listened. Then he said, "Don't let fear become your only advisor."

We returned home as the sun was lowering. The courtyard was warm. My mother was cooking. The smell of spices rose into the air and made my stomach tighten with hunger. Hunger, I learned, is a kind of truth. It does not care about speeches or flags.

I asked my grandfather, "Why are people afraid if we are free?"

He looked at me for a long moment, as if choosing the version of truth a boy could hold.

"Because freedom means you cannot blame someone else for everything," he said. "Now the choices are ours. And choices are heavy."

That was the first time I understood weight as something other than physical. Something invisible that still made people stoop.

It was around that time that I began to notice the way adults used silence differently.

My father used silence to avoid conflict. If a topic made him uncomfortable, he became loud in other ways, turning attention elsewhere. He was not dishonest; he was evasive. It is a form of self-protection.

My mother used silence to keep peace. She withheld words not because she didn't have them, but because she knew words could set fires. She saved language for moments when it mattered.

My grandfather used silence as a form of power. He waited. He listened. He let others empty themselves before he spoke, and when he spoke, people treated his words as if they had weight.

And me?

I began to use silence as a way to understand the room.

To survive a large family, you learn quickly what is safe to say and what is safer to keep inside. You learn how to read faces. You learn how to predict storms. You learn how to help without being asked because help, offered early, prevents conflict later.

Those were small lessons. Domestic lessons.

But they mirrored what was happening in the country.

India had gained independence, but independence did not automatically create harmony. It created responsibility. It created new conflicts. It forced people to reveal who they were when there was no longer an external ruler to point to.

A nation, I would later understand, grows the way a boy grows: awkwardly, unevenly, with bursts of pride and sudden insecurity. It does not become stable because it wants to. It becomes stable because people do the unglamorous work of stability.

That work was happening in our house too.

My father, despite his love of fun, still shouldered the duties of being eldest. He handled disputes, managed finances when needed, accompanied elders to appointments, made decisions that made him unpopular. There were days he looked tired in a way he couldn't laugh away.

My mother never looked surprised by difficulty. She moved through it the way water moves through rock: patient, persistent, reshaping the day without announcing the effort.

My grandfather continued doing what he always did: teach, guide, prepare. His theology was not ornamental. It was practical. It told him to care for people, yes, but also to build systems so caring didn't depend on mood.

When I think of those years, I do not remember dramatic events. I remember the daily rehearsal of responsibility.

I remember being asked to fetch water and doing it quickly because my mother needed it now. I remember being told to sit quietly when elders spoke and doing it, even when my legs wanted to run. I remember learning that my voice mattered less than the mood of the room.

And in 1947, I remember something else: the first time I felt pride that did not come from personal achievement.

It came from belonging to something larger.

The flag. The word "free." The brightness in people's faces. The sense that the future had widened by a few inches.

But pride, I learned, is not enough. It doesn't feed a family. It doesn't keep peace. It doesn't stop rumors from spreading or fear from multiplying.

What keeps things together is quieter.

It is the mother who cooks when everyone is anxious.

It is the grandfather who speaks calmly when others panic.

It is the eldest son who shows up even when he wants to escape.

It is the child who learns to listen before he speaks.

That was where my life began: in a house full of people, in a country full of uncertainty, learning that stability is rarely loud.

In those years, something was forming in me, though no one named it.

I was learning to hold.

I was learning to carry small responsibilities without applause. To notice what others needed before they asked. To sense what was coming and prepare quietly. To keep my own feelings contained so the room could stay calm.

Some boys learn to fight. Some boys learn to perform. I learned to pay attention.

I learned that silence is not weakness.

It is preparation.

I did not know then that one day I would become a father. That I would be asked to hold a different kind of weight—someone else's pain, someone else's fear, someone else's darkness. I did not know that my love would be tested not by how much I could provide, but by how much I could endure without control.

I only knew this:

India was learning to stand.

And I was learning to stand with it.

Freedom did not remove weight. It redistributed it.

That was the beginning.

Not of a nation. The nation had always existed in its people.

The beginning of a man learning what it meant to be a refuge—quietly, imperfectly, and without expecting recognition.

That was how I learned silence.

And that was how I learned my first truth:

A life is not built by the moments we celebrate.

It is built by the moments we hold.

CHAPTER 2

The Shape of Weight

Responsibility is a form of gravity. You feel it long before you understand its source.

By the time I understood the rules of our house, I already knew which ones could not be spoken.

In a joint family, rules are not written down. They are not explained. They are absorbed, the way heat settles into stone during the long summer months. You learn them not because someone teaches you, but because the cost of violating them is immediate and memorable. A raised eyebrow. A long pause. A story retold later with your mistake folded into it, quietly, permanently.

Our house was never empty.

It was never quiet.

It was never still.

Seven brothers. One sister. Their wives. Their children. Elders who sat at the center of everything like load-bearing pillars. Everyone had a place, and everyone knew where they stood in relation to everyone else, even if no one ever said it aloud.

Privacy was not a right. It was an accident.

If someone argued, everyone heard it. If someone worried, the worry traveled through the house like heat, touching meals, sleep, conversation. If someone failed, the failure did not stay contained. It spilled outward, altering the tone of the day, tightening the air, shifting how people spoke to one another.

As a child, I did not question this. It was simply the shape of the world.

Mornings began before the sun. They always had.

Someone was always awake before light. A broom scratched rhythmic lines into the courtyard dust. The water was heated. Ash cleared from the stove. The smell of smoke, milk, and grain mixed together into something that meant morning.

By the time the first light reached the courtyard, the house was already fully awake.

Elders claimed their places without discussion. Children adjusted instinctively. We learned how to pass behind someone without interrupting their conversation. We learned how to wait without asking how long. We learned how to become useful before being told.

Education mattered more than comfort.

That belief came from my grandfather, Pawan, and it survived him. School was not discussed as opportunity or ambition. It was spoken of as an obligation. You studied because the family fed you. You studied because the family needed someone who could navigate a changing world.

I discovered early that school came easily to me.

Mathematics felt natural, almost reassuring. Numbers behaved. They followed rules. They did not pretend. A problem either resolved or it didn't. There was no ambiguity about effort or outcome.

Physics, when it arrived later, felt like a deeper version of the same truth. Motion. Force. Balance. Cause and effect. The world explained without sentiment. The universe did not care how you felt, only whether you understood its laws.

I liked that.

Teachers noticed. They praised me cautiously, as if aware that praise could become a burden in a family already heavy with expectation. Relatives spoke of my "future" in vague terms that made me uneasy. Promise is a dangerous word. It invites comparison. It creates pressure where none is needed.

At home, I drew.

I drew whenever I could find a scrap of paper and a pencil short enough to be left alone. I copied what I saw. At first, lines and shapes. Then faces. Then scenes from memory—the courtyard at different hours, my mother's hands kneading dough, my grandfather seated with papers spread around him.

Drawing gave me something rare: solitude without isolation.

No one encouraged it as a future profession. No one discouraged it either. In a house where space and time were always borrowed, drawing was tolerated because it did not disrupt anyone else's needs.

I became known as the quiet one.

Not shy. Observant. Teachers said it kindly. Relatives said it with curiosity. "He is always thinking," they would say, as if thinking were a place I went alone.

Being quiet had advantages.

Adults forgot you were listening. They spoke freely. They revealed worries they did not intend to share. Money. Pride. Fear. Failure. I learned early that adults are rarely as certain as they appear.

That was how I learned about money.

After independence, the country continued to rearrange itself. Nationalism was no longer a slogan. It became policy. One of the most consequential changes was the nationalization of insurance. The argument was simple and persuasive: insurance was too important to be left in private hands. It should belong to the nation.

For men like my grandfather, the shift was not ideological.

It was immediate.

The business he had built—slowly, ethically, over decades—began to evaporate. Clients were reassigned. Policies transferred. Income stopped. What had once been reliable became uncertain almost overnight.

Evenings changed.

Conversations lingered longer on figures. Numbers were revisited repeatedly, as if repetition might change outcomes. My grandfather remained calm, but I noticed how long he sat with papers spread out before him, how often he pressed his fingers to his temples.

My father, Sanad, grew quieter.

He had always believed that goodwill could smooth most difficulties. He liked laughter. He liked lightness. He liked the idea that problems could be talked down if everyone stayed reasonable.

But reason does not replace income.

Then came the accident.

I was about ten. There was a tree near the edge of our neighborhood that children had claimed as their own. We climbed it because it was there. Because height offered perspective. Because for a few minutes, you could look down on the world instead of being managed by it.

That day, I climbed higher than usual.

The bark scraped my palms. The branches thinned. Someone shouted something from below—encouragement or warning, I don't remember which.

I remember slipping.

The fall was fast. There was no time to be afraid. There was only sound—a dull, final sound—and then pain so sharp it emptied my lungs. I remember lying still, staring at the sky, unable to move.

The days that followed blurred together. The doctor's office. The smell of antiseptic. Bandages wrapped too tightly. My mother's face was composed but strained. My father was standing too still, as if movement might make things worse.

The bone healed.

Mostly.

When I stood again, when I walked again, something was wrong. My left leg was shorter—just enough to matter. Not enough to correct easily. Enough to be noticed.

The gait stayed.

At first, I tried to ignore it. Children adapt quickly. I learned how to walk so the difference was less obvious. I learned how to sit before someone suggested it. I learned how to accept help without appearing to need it.

I learned something else too.

Vulnerability changes the way the world looks at you.

Some people became kinder. Some became uncomfortable. A few became casually cruel. I withdrew further into myself.

School became a refuge. Books did not notice the way I walked. Numbers did not adjust out of pity. Physics did not concern itself with fairness.

Not long after, my grandfather died.

There was no spectacle. No prolonged illness. He weakened quietly and then he was gone. His absence was immediate—not emotional at first, but practical.

Without his income, without his authority, responsibility collapsed onto my father.

Sanad became the sole provider for a family that had never learned how to be small.

He tried.

He took on work. He managed accounts. He negotiated with brothers who had grown accustomed to relying on someone else's steadiness. Each conversation took something from him. Each compromise drained energy he did not have.

I saw it in his face. In the way his laughter thinned. In the way his shoulders slumped at night. In the way he stared at figures longer than necessary.

My mother absorbed more. That was her instinct. When pressure increased, she tightened her routine. She spoke less. She moved faster. She protected the children from conversations they were not meant to hear.

And then my sister eloped.

In those days, such a thing was almost unthinkable.

A daughter leaving without permission. Without ceremony. Without the careful choreography that preserved honor.

The house did not explode.

It collapsed inward.

Voices rose and then stopped. Doors closed more often. Conversations ended abruptly. My mother cried once, late at night, believing no one could hear. I heard.

My father aged visibly in those weeks.

Shame is heavier than anger. It lingers longer. It sits in the chest and steals breath.

He tried to manage the fallout—relatives, neighbors, explanations. Each conversation reopened the wound. Each justification drained him further.

I watched him closely. I was seventeen. Old enough to recognize fear in an adult's eyes.

The heart attack came without warning.

One moment he was there. The next, he wasn't.

Forty-five years old.

When he died, the house went quiet in a way I had never known. Not the listening silence of night. A hollow silence. A vacuum.

I stood at the edge of the room, my left leg aching faintly, as if my body were reminding me of everything I could not fix.

By then, I was seventeen.

A gifted student, they said.

A quiet boy.

A boy with promise.

A boy standing at the edge of a life he had not chosen.

Not with clarity.

With weight.

CHAPTER 3
The Loan

Sometimes a life changes direction because someone else decides to believe in it.

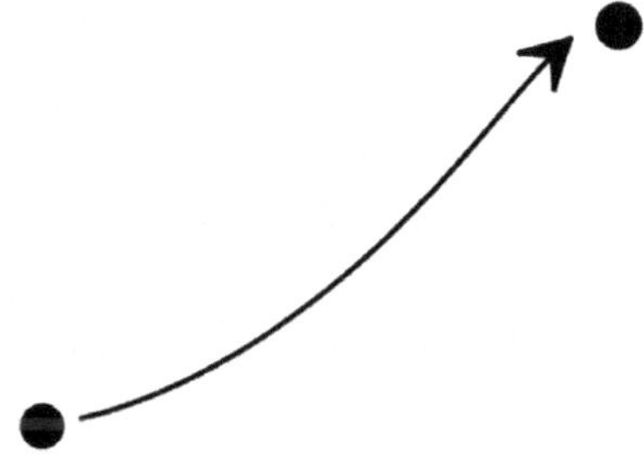

When my father died, the house did not collapse the way I expected.

It reorganized.

Grief moved in familiar channels. Someone brought water. Someone sent word to relatives. Someone spoke in a low voice about arrangements. Women gathered in the kitchen and did what women always did in our world when the men were broken, they fed the day back into motion.

I stood in the courtyard with my left leg aching faintly, watching strangers and relatives move through rooms that suddenly felt smaller. People spoke to me more carefully than before. Softer. As if carefulness could protect me from what had already happened.

I was seventeen.

A boy who had been told he had promise.

A boy whose promise now had to compete with reality.

There are certain losses that do not feel like sadness at first. They feel like accounting. You begin to count what has disappeared: income, stability, authority, protection. You begin to count what remains: mouths to feed, fees to pay, debts to manage, reputations to preserve.

My grandfather was gone. My father was gone. The insurance business that had once given us confidence had dried up into memory. And the joint family—our sprawling, complicated ecosystem—did what it always did under pressure.

It looked for the next beam.

People began to look at me.

Not dramatically. Not with a declaration. Just in small ways. A question asked of me instead of my mother. An errand assigned to me without apology. A silence that waited for my response.

I hated it.

Not because I didn't want responsibility. I had been raised on it. I hated it because I could feel how unprepared I was. Seventeen is an age where you still believe you are allowed to become someone. Suddenly I was expected to already be someone.

The day after the funeral rituals were complete, I returned to school.

Not out of courage. Out of instinct.

School was the one place where the rules made sense. A problem had a solution. A circuit did what it did. A theorem did not care about grief. In a world that had become unpredictable, equations remained loyal.

Teachers offered condolences. Classmates looked at me with the awkward kindness people reserve for tragedy. I nodded, thanked them, kept my eyes lowered, and went back to my work.

At home, my mother moved as if she had been carved into routine.

Karma did not dramatize loss. She handled it. She tightened the household's order the way a person tightens a cloth around a wound. She woke earlier. She spoke less. She became more precise, as if precision could reduce waste.

Some relatives suggested that I should stop studying. Take work. Help immediately.

Others suggested I should study harder than ever. That education was the only ladder left.

Both sides were correct. That was the cruelty of it.

One evening, after a day that had already been too long, a man came to our house.

Yadu.

He was my father's close friend—close enough that he had been present at celebrations and crises, close enough that his voice carried authority without being family. He had the kind of calm that made a room settle. He did not speak loudly. He did not offer unnecessary comfort. He looked at my mother, then at me, and sat down as if he belonged there.

He spoke about my father first. Not in poetic terms. In practical ones.

"Sanad was a good man," he said. "He tried."

My mother nodded. Her eyes remained steady.

Then Yadu looked at me.

"You are still in school," he said.

It wasn't a question. It was a statement that carried expectation.

"Yes," I said.

"Good," he replied. "You will continue."

Something about the way he said it made me feel both relieved and trapped. Relieved that someone had made a decision. Trapped because that decision now came with a debt I didn't know how to repay.

In the days that followed, Yadu began appearing more often. Not daily. Not intrusively. Just enough that his presence became a new kind of structure. Sometimes he came in the evening and spoke with my mother. Sometimes he asked me about my classes. Sometimes he sat quietly for a few minutes and then left, as if his job was simply to remind the house that it was not alone.

No one called him my guardian. No one spoke of "mentorship." But that is what it was.

An unspoken father-son relationship, formed not from sentiment but from necessity.

Yadu did not touch my shoulder or speak in grand encouragement. He did not tell me to be strong. He told me to be consistent.

"Study," he said once, when I hesitated about spending time on a difficult topic. "You do not have the luxury of being average."

He said it as a fact, not an insult.

He was right.

I studied the way a drowning person learns to breathe. I studied because it was the only direction that didn't feel like surrender. At night, when the house quieted, I sat with books and papers, the sounds of the household drifting through walls—someone coughing, someone turning, my mother moving in the kitchen one last time.

I learned to work through fatigue. I learned to ignore hunger. I learned to let my left leg ache without complaint. I learned to accept that some days my mind would feel heavy, and I would have to move it anyway.

When I received my acceptance to engineering school in Hubli, I did not celebrate.

I stared at the paper the way you stare at a door you are not sure you deserve to walk through.

Hubli felt far enough to be a different life. It also felt impossible.

Tuition. Books. Travel. Living expenses.

My mother said little when I showed her the letter. She read it carefully, once, then again, then placed it down on the table as if it were fragile.

"You should go," she said.

Her voice did not shake. That was my mother's strength. She did not offer permission with emotion. She offered it as a duty.

But I saw the calculation behind her eyes. How much could she spare? What would the family say? What debts would this create?

When Yadu came that evening, my mother handed him the letter without explanation.

He read it, nodded once, and then looked at me.

"You will go," he said.

Again, not a suggestion. A decision.

I didn't know how to respond. Gratitude and shame arrived together. In our world, receiving help is complicated. It makes you small. It makes you dependent. It makes you feel like your future is being purchased by someone else's generosity.

Yadu reached into his pocket and removed a small notebook. He flipped it open, wrote something, tore out a page, and placed it on the table.

It was a number.

Enough to cover tuition and expenses for the first stretch.

A loan.

Not charity.

That distinction mattered to both of us. It allowed my dignity to remain intact. It gave me a way to repay, to restore balance.

“I will return it,” I said quickly.

Yadu looked at me as if I had said something obvious.

“You will,” he said. “Not because you are proud. Because you are capable.”

That was all.

No lecture. No moral speech. Just a transaction wrapped in trust.

Hubli did not greet me with ceremony. Hubli did not feel like freedom. It felt like weight with a different shape.

The campus was larger than anything I had known. The classrooms smelled of chalk and sweat and ambition. The boys around me came from families with stability—fathers who could pay tuition without hesitation, mothers who could send sweets without counting costs.

The first night I arrived, I stood outside the hostel building with a small trunk and a folded blanket under my arm. The building was older than I expected. Paint peeling. Windows slightly crooked. The air smelled faintly of iron and damp paper.

A boy from another room helped carry my trunk up the stairs. He did not ask about my limp. He did not ask about my family. He asked only what branch I was in.

“Electrical,” I said.

He nodded as if that explained everything.

The room was small—two beds, two desks, one narrow window. I ran my hand over the desk before placing my books down. It felt like claiming territory. Not ownership—just a temporary claim.

That first night, sleep did not come easily.

I lay on the thin mattress and listened to the unfamiliar sounds of young men adjusting to shared space. Someone snored. Someone coughed. Someone whispered long after the lights were out. I realized that this was the first time I had left the orbit of my family completely.

Freedom did not feel light.

It felt exposed.

The next morning, I walked to the campus courtyard early. My left leg had stiffened overnight. It always did when I was anxious. I adjusted my pace until the gait felt less pronounced.

Engineering classes began without ceremony. No welcome speech about destiny. No acknowledgment that some of us had arrived from collapse. Just chalk on board. Circuits drawn. Problems assigned.

I felt immediate relief.

There is something merciful about structured work when your internal world is unsettled. If you focus on resistance, voltage, and current, grief has fewer openings.

But grief did not disappear.

Some nights, after hours of study, I would feel it quietly—not as tears, but as a tightening behind the ribs. I would think of my father sitting alone in the courtyard. I would think of my mother moving through rooms without pause. I would think of Yadu's notebook, the number written carefully on the page.

Debt sharpens discipline.

Every problem I solved felt like partial repayment. Every exam passed felt like an installment returned.

Letters from home arrived irregularly. My mother's handwriting was neat, careful. She wrote about the price of grain. About a cousin's illness. About a roof repair that could not wait.

She did not write about loneliness.

Between her lines, I read what was not written.

Once, in the middle of a semester, I considered returning home. The thought came suddenly, after reading a letter that mentioned a new expense. I imagined walking back into the courtyard and telling my mother I would find work locally. That I would postpone the rest.

That evening, Yadu appeared at the hostel without warning.

I do not know how he timed it. Perhaps it was a coincidence. Perhaps it was instinct.

He sat on the edge of the narrow bed and looked around the room. Books stacked neatly. Papers arranged in order. Shoes aligned under the desk.

"You are thinking of coming back," he said.

It was not a question.

I did not answer.

He leaned back slightly, crossing his arms.

"If you return now," he said, "you will not solve the problem. You will multiply it."

I felt something tighten in my chest.

"You think staying is selfish," he continued. "It is not. It is structural."

That word stayed with me.

Structural.

He was not asking me to be brave. He was asking me to be strategic.

"You will repay this," he said quietly. "But not by abandoning it."

He stood to leave. No embrace. No dramatics.

After he left, I sat at my desk and opened my notebook.

That night, I studied harder than I had before.

I learned quickly not to speak much about my background. Not out of shame, exactly. Out of fatigue. Explaining loss requires energy, and I needed my energy for study.

Engineering suited me. Not just because I was good at mathematics and physics, but because it offered a kind of order. Circuits, systems, signals—everything had logic. Even when it was complex, it was honest. If something failed, you could trace the failure. You could diagnose it. You could correct it.

Life was not like that. But engineering was.

I flourished.

Not in a dramatic way. Quietly. Consistently. I attended lectures, took notes, asked questions only when necessary. I spent long hours with books, with diagrams, with problems that refused to yield until I gave them full attention.

Sometimes, late at night, I would sketch.

Not because art had become important again, but because sketching was the only way I knew to rest without wasting time. A pencil and paper. A face remembered. A street scene. The curve of a circuit diagram rendered with unnecessary beauty.

There was something soothing in lines that obeyed your hand.

My leg remained a companion. In the crowded hallways, people noticed the gait. Some asked. Most didn't. In college, everyone carried something—ambition, insecurity, hunger. My limp was simply one visible version of what others hid.

I learned to walk quickly anyway. To arrive on time. To not ask for accommodation. I had become good at adjusting myself to the world rather than asking the world to adjust to me.

Letters came from home. My mother's writing was brief. Practical. Updates about relatives, about money, about the slow churn of survival. Yadu rarely wrote, but when he did, his words were few and direct.

"Focus," he wrote once. "Do not waste this."

As if waste were a sin.

I graduated with high distinction.

When the results came, I stared at the marks in disbelief. It wasn't the pride I felt first. It was a relief. Relief that I had not betrayed Yadu's trust. Relief that my father's death had not ended our trajectory completely. Relief that something in my life was moving forward.

The scholarship to pursue graduate work in electrical engineering in Pune arrived like another door.

A bigger door.

College of Engineering in Pune was a top school. People spoke of it with respect. The kind of respect that suggested you were now entering rooms where futures were made more formally.

Again, I did not celebrate.

I did the same accounting. Tuition. Living expenses. Travel. Books.

And again, Yadu appeared.

He did not announce his help. He did not frame it as a sacrifice. He simply did what needed doing.

"You will go," he said.

By then, I had learned not to argue. Not because I had become comfortable receiving. Because I had begun to understand what Yadu was doing.

He was not just supporting me.

He was continuing my father.

Not in the sentimental sense. In the structural sense. He was making sure the roof did not collapse simply because one beam had fallen.

Pune was different.

Hubli had been earnest. Pune was competitive.

The campus carried prestige like an invisible badge. Students moved quickly. Conversations were sharper. Intelligence was not rare here — it was assumed.

For the first time, I was no longer the obvious top student in every room.

At first, this unsettled me. I had built part of my identity around competence. In Pune, competence was baseline.

But something else happened.

I discovered that what set me apart was not brilliance. It was endurance.

Many students were quick thinkers. They solved problems in bursts of insight. I solved them by staying longer. By refusing to leave a question incomplete. By revisiting fundamentals until the structure was clear.

Grief had trained me for this.

Responsibility had trained me for this.

There were evenings when classmates gathered in groups, laughing, debating politics, discussing futures abroad. I sometimes joined them. Often, I did not. I preferred the quiet library corners, the predictable hum of fluorescent lights, the slow certainty of work accumulating.

One professor noticed.

"You are disciplined," he said once after class. "That will carry you further than speed."

It was the closest thing to praise that mattered.

Financial strain did not disappear. Even with scholarship support, expenses lingered. I budgeted carefully. I ate simply. I sent money home when possible, though small.

Yadu wrote less now. Not because he cared less. Because he trusted more.

Trust is another form of investment.

In Pune, I learned that intelligence is common and discipline is rare.

Many students were brilliant. Many could solve problems quickly. But fewer could remain consistent when the problems became tedious, when the days became long, when no one was watching.

Consistency had been my inheritance.

Grief had taught it to me. The joint family had trained it into me. Poverty had sharpened it. Yadu had demanded it.

I worked harder than ever. I studied systems, signals, and machines. I learned to think in layers—inputs, outputs, constraints. I began to understand how electricity could be shaped, controlled, harnessed.

Sometimes, when I walked across campus, the sun low and the air cooling, I felt something unfamiliar.

Hope.

Not optimism. Not fantasy.

Hope as a quiet sense that life might not only be survival. That it could include stability, dignity, perhaps even joy.

After Pune, an engagement in Goa came. When the offer came for a teaching engagement in Goa, I hesitated.

Teaching felt different from engineering design. It felt less ambitious. But it also felt stable.

The idea startled me at first. I had always imagined engineering as building, designing, producing. Teaching felt like stepping sideways rather than forward.

But there was something in it that appealed to me. The structure of a classroom. The clean exchange of knowledge. The way a student's confusion could become clear if you guided them patiently.

Stability was no longer something I dismissed.

I accepted.

In Goa, I learned a different kind of discipline, the discipline of being responsible for others' understanding.

You cannot hide behind brilliance when you teach. You must be clear. You must be patient. You must care.

I wrote to my mother. I sent money when I could. I continued to hold the invisible ledger in my mind—the debt to Yadu, the responsibility to my family, the need to remain upright.

When Yadu visited me in Goa and spoke Sunita's name, something shifted in the room.

I had known his daughters as children—polite, distant, moving through rooms with the quiet awareness that daughters must learn early.

Sunita.

The name carried no drama in my memory. No hidden affection. No secret glances.

Which made the proposal honest.

Yadu did not describe her beauty. He did not speak of compatibility. He did not sell the idea.

He simply said, "You have been alone too long."

I did not immediately answer.

Marriage was not a romantic decision in our world. It was structural. It created continuity. It extended the obligation. It bound families together in ways that could not be undone easily.

I thought about my limp. About the way I walked into rooms and people noticed. I thought about the debt I still carried, even if unspoken. I thought about my mother aging quietly at home.

"Does she agree?" I asked.

Yadu's eyes softened slightly.

"She does."

The simplicity of that answer mattered.

I did not want to be chosen out of gratitude. I did not want to be offered as repayment.

I wanted mutual dignity.

That night, alone in my small quarters, I imagined a life that was not defined solely by recovery. A house not burdened by collapse. A partner who did not see me as a project but as a person.

I did not feel excited.

I felt steadiness.

The next day, when Yadu asked again, I said yes.

Not impulsively. Not reluctantly.

Deliberately.

Marriage did not feel like escape.

It felt like alignment.

Yadu nodded once, as if the decision had already been made and my answer was simply confirmation.

"Good," he said. "We will speak to your mother."

Later, alone, I sat on the edge of my bed and tried to understand what I had agreed to.

Marriage.

A new responsibility.

A new roof.

I thought about my life up to that point. How it had been shaped by loss, by obligation, by the steady presence of people who did not make speeches about love but enacted it anyway.

I had lost my grandfather. I had lost my father. I had lost the easy confidence of childhood. I had gained a limp, a scholarship, a career, a mentor, a debt.

And now, I was being offered something that felt like more than opportunity.

A future that was not solely mine to carry.

That night, I did not sleep quickly.

I stared at the ceiling and felt the familiar weight in my chest. But for the first time, the weight did not feel like the only burden.

It felt like direction.

It felt like a hand placed quietly on your shoulder—not guiding you with force, but reminding you that you were no longer alone.

That is how my adult life began.

Not with freedom.

With a loan.

With trust.

With a man who became my father without ever using the word.

And with Sunita's name, spoken once, calmly, as if it had always been waiting for its place in my story.

CHAPTER 4
A Household in Bhopal

Stability does not arrive as an event. It grows quietly from shared responsibility.

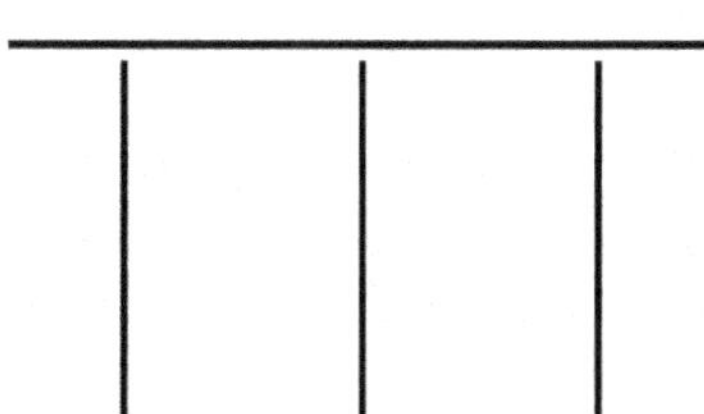

The morning of my wedding began earlier than I expected.

Not because there was noise or celebration, but because sleep had abandoned me before dawn. I lay awake on a thin mattress in a room that smelled faintly of sandalwood and starch, staring at a ceiling fan that moved slowly, as if reluctant to disturb the air.

Marriage had arrived quietly.

There had been no courtship, no elaborate exchange of letters, no private conversations under moonlight. In our world, marriage was rarely the result of romance. It was the result of alignment—families, timing, circumstances.

Sometimes it was simply a convenience.

Sometimes it was destiny.

Most often it was what came next.

Yadu had spoken Sunita's name calmly, as if placing a piece on a board where it had always belonged. I had said yes with the same calmness. The decision had not felt dramatic. It had felt structural.

Now, lying awake before the rituals began, I realized something strange: I did not feel nervous about marriage itself.

What unsettled me was the possibility of stability.

For years my life had been shaped by loss and recovery — grandfather gone, father gone, the family finances shrinking like a river in summer. Responsibility had come early and stayed heavy.

Marriage meant something different.

It meant that responsibility would now be shared.

That idea was unfamiliar.

The wedding itself passed in a blur of ritual.

Relatives moved in coordinated patterns around us, adjusting fabrics, whispering instructions, correcting gestures that had been repeated for generations. The priest spoke verses whose meanings I understood only partially, but whose cadence carried authority.

Sunita sat beside me, calm in a way that surprised me.

I had seen her only a few times before—always in brief encounters during visits to Yadu's home. I knew she had completed her medical degree. I knew she was disciplined, serious about her work, and not inclined toward unnecessary conversation.

Now she sat quietly beside me as garlands were exchanged and sacred fire circled.

There was no theatrical smile on her face. No shyness meant for display.

Instead there was something steadier.

Composure.

When our eyes met briefly during the ceremony, there was no embarrassment. Just acknowledgement—two people agreeing to step into the same direction.

After the rituals ended, after the elders had offered blessings and the crowd began to thin, Yadu placed his hand on my shoulder.

"You have built yourself well," he said quietly.

Then he looked toward Sunita.

"Now build together."

Those words stayed with me long after the wedding ended.

Our new life began in Bhopal.

The decision was not accidental.

During my graduate work and early teaching, I had discovered that academia suited me in ways I had not expected. The rhythm of teaching, the clarity of engineering concepts, the discipline of research — all of it felt natural.

When an opportunity appeared for an assistant professorship in electrical engineering at the Maulana Azad College of Technology in Bhopal, I accepted.

The name itself carried weight.

Maulana Azad College of Technology—M.A.C.T., as everyone called it — had been established to cultivate engineers for a country that was still building itself. India was young as a nation, ambitious and uncertain. Institutions like MACT were meant to shape the people who would design its infrastructure.

To be part of that effort felt meaningful.

Bhopal greeted us with a landscape very different from the places I had lived before.

The city unfolded around water.

Two large lakes defined its geography — the Upper Lake stretching wide like a sheet of silver under the sun, the Lower Lake nestled closer to the old city. In the mornings, mist hovered above the water as fishermen moved quietly in narrow boats. By afternoon the light sharpened, reflecting off the lake's surface in bright fragments.

The city itself was a meeting point of histories.

Old Bhopal carried the imprint of princely rule—narrow lanes, domed mosques, markets dense with color and noise. New Bhopal spread outward with wider roads and government buildings, the architecture of a nation reorganizing itself.

Between those worlds stood MACT.

The campus lay away from the busiest parts of the city, spread across open land where dusty roads connected academic blocks, laboratories, and staff quarters. The buildings were practical rather than beautiful—long corridors, tall windows, concrete staircases that echoed when students moved between classes.

But there was energy there.

Students arrived from different parts of the country—some from cities, others from towns even smaller than the one I had grown up in. They carried ambition in their notebooks and uncertainty in their posture.

Many were the first engineers their families had ever produced.

I understood that feeling.

Sunita and I moved into the staff quarters assigned to young faculty.

The house was modest—three rooms, a small kitchen, a narrow veranda facing a dusty path where bicycles passed regularly. In the evenings the sound of students laughing drifted through open windows.

For the first time in years, I was living in a house that did not feel temporary.

Sunita arranged the kitchen with quiet efficiency.

She had begun her own journey in Bhopal as well. After completing her M.B.B.S., she had secured a residency in pharmacology at Mahatma Gandhi Medical College (GMC). It was not the path she might have chosen independently—she might have preferred another city, another specialization—but marriage had introduced new coordinates to her life.

Neither of us spoke about sacrifice.

Instead we spoke about logistics.

Her hospital schedule was demanding. Long hours. Night duties. Endless rounds where senior doctors expected discipline from their residents.

My academic routine, though structured, was hardly light.

A typical day began early.

I woke before sunrise, often out of habit formed during years of study. The air in Bhopal at that hour carried a softness that disappeared by midday. I would review lecture notes while drinking tea Sunita prepared before leaving for the hospital.

By eight, I was walking toward the campus.

The roads around MACT filled quickly with students on bicycles, their bags slung over shoulders, notebooks pressed under arms. Some greeted me respectfully as they passed. Others pedaled faster, anxious about arriving late to class.

Teaching electrical engineering demanded clarity.

Unlike subjects that allowed room for interpretation, engineering insisted on precision. A circuit either worked or it did not. A calculation either held or collapsed.

I enjoyed the challenge.

Standing in front of a classroom, chalk in hand, I felt a familiar calm settle over me. The blackboard became a place where complexity could be reduced to structure — lines representing current flow, equations describing relationships that governed invisible forces.

Students asked questions hesitantly at first.

Over time they grew more confident. A good question often revealed the deeper confusion beneath a concept. I welcomed those moments.

After lectures, I spent hours in the laboratory guiding students through practical experiments—measuring voltages, testing circuits, troubleshooting systems that refused to behave as theory predicted.

Engineering education in those years required patience.

Equipment was limited. Instruments malfunctioned. Sometimes we improvised with tools that would have embarrassed more developed institutions.

But there was pride in the effort.

We were building something.

Sunita's days were longer than mine.

Her residency consumed time in ways that academic schedules did not. She often returned late, her white coat folded over her arm, exhaustion visible even when she tried to hide it.

Yet she rarely complained.

Instead she described the day in fragments—a complicated case, a difficult senior doctor, a pharmacology concept she found fascinating.

Medicine demanded a different kind of attention than engineering.

Where I dealt with systems, she dealt with bodies—fragile, unpredictable, carrying lives that could not be reset like circuits.

Sometimes we sat together late at night, both working quietly — she reviewing medical texts, I preparing lecture material.

Those evenings felt strangely peaceful.

Our conversations were simple.

What to cook the next day. Whether a new fan was needed for the bedroom. Whether the monsoon would arrive early that year.

Small decisions, but shared.

Not long after we settled in Bhopal, my mother joined us.

Karma arrived with a single trunk and the quiet authority she had always carried. Traditionally, the eldest son's household absorbed the responsibility of caring for aging parents. I was not the eldest.

But tradition bends when necessity demands it.

My elder brother had his own struggles. His household was already stretched thin. No one spoke the decision aloud, but it was understood.

My mother would live with us.

Sunita accepted the arrangement without outward hesitation.

She greeted Karma with respect that went beyond obligation. In the small kitchen they quickly developed a rhythm—cooking together, sharing responsibilities, occasionally disagreeing about spices in ways that ended with quiet laughter.

Watching them, I felt something settle inside me.

For years our family had felt like a structure missing key beams. Now, slowly, something resembling stability was returning.

With stability came responsibility.

I found myself assuming roles my father had once carried—managing finances, making decisions for relatives who still turned to me for guidance, balancing the expectations of family with the demands of academic life.

Sometimes the weight felt familiar.

Other times it surprised me.

But unlike the chaos that followed my father's death, this responsibility now rested within a household that functioned.

Sunita's discipline anchored the home.

Karma's quiet strength preserved continuity.

And my work at MACT gave direction to the days.

Years passed with a rhythm that felt almost ordinary.

Lectures. Hospital rounds. Evenings on the veranda watching students cycle past. Occasional visits from Yadu, whose presence still carried the calm authority that had changed the course of my life.

India itself was changing during those years.

The country spoke often of development—new industries, dams, factories, institutions of learning. Engineers and doctors were seen as builders of the nation's future.

Sometimes, standing in the laboratory surrounded by students struggling to understand the behavior of electrical systems, I felt the weight of that expectation.

But mostly I felt something simpler.

Gratitude.

In 1971, our family changed again.

Sunita gave birth to our first child—a daughter.

The hospital corridor outside the delivery room smelled sharply of antiseptic. Doctors moved quickly. Nurses spoke in efficient bursts of instruction. I stood awkwardly near the doorway, aware that this world belonged more to Sunita than to me.

When the nurse finally emerged carrying a small bundle wrapped in cloth, she smiled briefly.

"A girl," she said.

I held my daughter for the first time with hands that suddenly felt too large, too uncertain.

She was impossibly small.

Her face moved in tiny expressions as if she were already reacting to a world she had just entered. When she opened her eyes briefly, they seemed unfocused, searching for something she could not yet understand.

We named her Sarla.

That night, sitting beside Sunita's hospital bed, watching Sarla sleep in the small crib near the wall, I felt a quiet shift inside me.

For years I had carried the memory of collapse—a house that had lost its pillars, a family struggling to remain upright.

Now, holding my daughter's tiny hand, I realized that the story had changed.

Responsibility was no longer only inheritance.

It was a creation.

And as I sat there in the dim hospital room in Bhopal, listening to the distant sounds of the city settling into night, I understood something simple.

The life that had once felt like recovery had become something else.

It had become a beginning.

CHAPTER 5

The Other Side of Stability

The years that appear ordinary while we live them often become the ones that shape us most.

Karan was born on a hot midnight in 1974.

The hospital corridors in Bhopal were quieter that day than they had been when Sarla was born three years earlier. Perhaps I had grown used to the rhythm of hospitals through Sunita's years of residency, or perhaps the second child simply felt less like an event and more like a continuation.

Still, when the nurse placed the child in my arms, I noticed immediately that he was different.

Sarla had arrived into the world calmly, as if she had studied the situation beforehand and decided it was acceptable.

Karan arrived like a challenge.

Even as a newborn his eyes moved constantly, scanning the room with restless curiosity. When he cried, it was loud and impatient, as if the world had already failed to meet his expectations.

Sunita smiled faintly when she saw my expression.

"This one will not be easy," she said.

She was right.

By the time Karan was born, I had spent three years teaching electrical engineering at MACT.

Academia suited my mind.

Teaching forced clarity. Research required patience. Writing papers gave structure to thought. The campus environment—bicycles moving through dusty paths, students debating problems under trees—felt like a small republic of ideas.

But ideas do not pay school fees.

When the offer arrived from Bharat Heavy Electricals Limited (BHEL), I read the letter several times before speaking to Sunita.

BHEL was expanding rapidly. The Indian government had invested heavily in heavy industry, and Bhopal had become one of the central manufacturing centers for power equipment.

The salary was significantly higher.

The decision was not philosophical.

It was arithmetic.

One evening after dinner I showed the letter to Sunita.

She read it carefully, the way she read everything—once for meaning, once for implication.

"You should take it," she said simply.

There was no hesitation in her voice.

We both understood what the decision meant.

Academia had been my preference.

Industry would become my responsibility.

The BHEL township was unlike anything I had seen before.

It was not just a workplace. It was an ecosystem.

Factories stretched across enormous compounds where turbines, generators, and massive industrial components were assembled with a scale that felt almost intimidating. Beyond the factory gates, the township unfolded like a carefully planned city.

Apartment blocks lined broad roads shaded by neem and gulmohar trees. Schools, markets, parks, and medical facilities existed within walking distance. Buses moved employees between residential sectors and factory complexes.

Nearly 20,000 employees worked there.

With families included, the population approac**hed 50,000 people.**

A city within a city.

Our apartment was modest—a three-bedroom flat in a row of identical buildings painted a shade of pale government beige. The walls were thin, the balconies narrow, but the layout allowed something we had not enjoyed before.

Space.

Sunita set up her study table near a window where afternoon light fell evenly across her books. My desk occupied a corner of the living room, stacked with engineering manuals, notebooks, and loose sheets filled with calculations.

Karma immediately took control of the kitchen.

Her presence anchored the household in ways I had come to rely upon without realizing it.

If Sunita and I were the visible structure of the household, Karma was its foundation.

Age had softened her movements but sharpened her stillness. She had begun to immerse herself more deeply in spiritual practice—long morning prayers, occasional temple visits, and hours spent reading scriptures whose meanings she rarely discussed.

But spirituality had not distanced her from the practical world.

She cooked. She organized the house. She watched over Sarla and later Karan with a patience that seemed endless.

Children have an instinct for unconditional love.

Both of them gravitated toward her.

Sarla, always obedient, followed instructions carefully and asked questions only when she had thought through them first.

Karan behaved differently.

He tested boundaries.

If Karma asked him not to climb the compound wall, he would climb it again the next day—slightly higher.

If Sarla completed her homework early, Karan would finish half of his and then wander outside to investigate something more interesting.

Yet Karma never scolded him harshly.

She simply watched.

"He is searching," she once said quietly.

Karan's searching often involved risk.

One afternoon when he was about eight or nine, a group of neighborhood children gathered near a shallow rain-fed pond not far from our apartment blocks.

The monsoon had filled the depression with muddy water, and the children had discovered the ancient sport of skipping stones across the surface.

As Karan recounted his story later, when I found him in the house hiding under the bed, he had watched the older boys carefully.

He bent his arm back, imitating their motion, and launched the stone across the water.

The pebble skipped twice before striking another boy near the eye.

The laughter stopped instantly.

The injured child began crying. Blood appeared quickly, shocking in its brightness against the muddy surroundings.

Karan froze.

I grabbed him by the ear, pulled him out from under the bed, and marched him across the compound toward the other boy's house.

"Apologize," I said firmly.

His voice trembled slightly as he repeated the words.

Decades later, I would learn that the boy he struck would remember the moment very differently—as the beginning of a friendship that lasted across continents.

At that moment, however, it was simply a lesson.

Stones thrown carelessly travel farther than we expect.

My work at BHEL was intellectually demanding.

Technically, the challenges were fascinating. The scale of engineering involved in power generation equipment pushed design and manufacturing capabilities constantly.

I enjoyed solving those problems.

What unsettled me was the environment surrounding them.

BHEL was a government enterprise, and with that came layers of bureaucracy that engineering alone could not solve. Decisions moved slowly through administrative hierarchies. Efficiency often yielded to politics.

There were times when technical logic lost to personal alliances.

I was not good at navigating such terrain.

Technically brilliant, some colleagues would say. Politically naive, others whispered more accurately.

Over time, I began withdrawing into the aspects of work I could control.

Engineering problems. Calculations. Writing.

Writing, especially, became an outlet.

I began drafting textbooks on electrical engineering topics — clear explanations for students who struggled with the same concepts I had once taught. The process felt familiar, almost like returning to academia through a side door.

Evenings often found me at my desk long after dinner, pages spread around me while the household slept.

Sunita's career moved along a different path.

After completing her residency, she joined the Department of Pharmacology at Gandhi Medical College as an assistant professor.

Government medical institutions carried their own bureaucratic challenges. Promotions moved slowly. Research funding was limited. Administrative procedures often seemed designed to test patience rather than efficiency.

Yet Sunita approached her work with relentless focus.

She began building a research program in pharmacology—modest at first, then gradually gaining recognition. Late nights at the dining table reviewing medical journals became common.

Eventually she pursued a PhD, balancing teaching responsibilities with research.

Her discipline impressed colleagues.

At home, however, another layer of emotion surfaced.

Sunita had grown up among sisters whose marriages had placed them in more affluent households. Occasionally, during rare quiet conversations, comparisons slipped into her voice.

"They travel more," she once remarked absentmindedly.

I said nothing.

Comparisons are natural in families, but they carry a subtle danger. They measure life against a scale that rarely reflects reality.

Still, I understood the tension.

Ambition had brought her into medicine.

Marriage had redirected its geography.

In 1983 something unexpected happened.

India won the Cricket World Cup.

The final was played at Lord's in England—the symbolic heart of cricket's colonial past. Few people believed India could defeat the mighty West Indies, whose dominance in world cricket had seemed almost permanent.

But they did.

The evening the match ended, the BHEL township erupted in celebration.

Radios blared commentary from open windows. Firecrackers appeared spontaneously. Men who rarely spoke to each other embraced in the streets.

I watched the celebrations from our balcony.

It was more than a sporting victory.

For a country still discovering its confidence, the triumph carried psychological weight. It suggested that the old hierarchies of the world could be challenged.

Even Karma, who had little interest in sports, smiled at the excitement spreading through the neighborhood.

For a moment, the entire nation seemed to breathe differently.

A year later, Bhopal experienced a different kind of night.

December 1984.

I woke before dawn to a strange feeling in the air—sharp, irritating, unfamiliar.

Within minutes the neighborhood stirred with confusion. People stepped outside, watching hordes of crowds escaping from something unseen. Some covered their faces with cloth. Others began running without direction.

Rumors spread quickly.

Gas leak.

Factory.

Danger.

The city descended into chaos.

From our balcony I saw families rushing through the streets, carrying children, shouting warnings that no one fully understood. The air burned the throat and eyes.

Inside the apartment, Sunita moved with controlled urgency.

"Close the windows," she said.

We soaked cloths in water and covered our faces. Sarla and Karan woke frightened but quiet, sensing the seriousness of the moment.

Hours later the scale of the disaster began to emerge.

The Union Carbide gas tragedy had released toxic methyl isocyanate into the night air. Thousands had been exposed while sleeping. Hospitals overflowed with victims struggling to breathe.

Sunita left immediately to assist at the medical college.

For days she returned home exhausted, her face lined with the strain of what she had witnessed.

Entire families were affected.

Children blinded.

Chaos overwhelming medical systems.

Bhopal would never feel the same again.

Even years later, when I walked through parts of the city, the memory of that night remained like a shadow that refused to lift.

Through these years Karan continued growing into the restless child Sunita had predicted.

School never bored him exactly.

It frustrated him.

Teachers noticed his intelligence quickly. Concepts came easily when he chose to engage. But consistency was not his strength.

Some days he returned home with perfect scores.

Other days he had forgotten assignments entirely.

By the age of nine something shifted. We later found out that it was the mentorship of Mr. Patole that changed Karan's trajectory.

He began reading constantly—science books, stories, anything that offered ideas beyond the classroom routine. The rebellious energy that once sent him climbing compound walls began redirecting itself toward curiosity.

Watching him, I sometimes felt a strange mixture of pride and concern.

Brilliance carries its own dangers.

Toward the end of the decade, another kind of change began unfolding far from Bhopal.

The Cold War—a geopolitical tension that had defined global politics since the Second World War—began loosening its grip.

In 1989 the word Perestroika entered global conversation.

Reforms in the Soviet Union suggested that a rigid system might be capable of transformation. For a generation that had grown up believing the world divided permanently between ideological camps, the moment felt historic.

In India, we watched these developments from a distance.

But even from that distance, something felt different.

Structures that once appeared immovable were shifting.

By 1989 Sarla was approaching adulthood.

Karan was moving toward adolescence.

Sunita had completed her PhD and established herself firmly in academic medicine.

Karma continued her daily prayers, her quiet presence still anchoring the household.

And I remained where circumstances had placed me — an engineer in industry who still thought like an academic, writing late into the night, trying to balance systems both electrical and human.

Looking back on those years, I realize they were not defined by dramatic turning points.

They were defined by accumulation.

Work. Children. Responsibility. Quiet compromises.

The long middle of a life—where the world outside changes constantly, while inside the house you simply continue building.

And sometimes, without realizing it, those ordinary years become the ones that shape everything that follows.

CHAPTER 6

The Difficult Son

A parent's task is not to choose a child's direction, but to remain steady while they discover it.

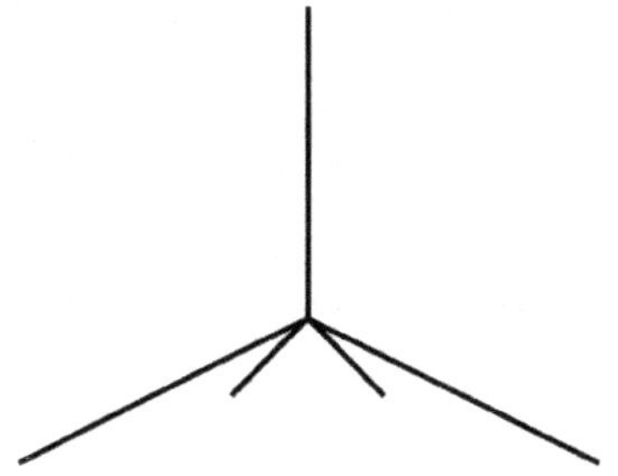

By the time Karan entered his teenage years, something inside me had begun to change.

It did not happen suddenly. There was no single event I could point to and say, this is where the shift began. Instead it was like the slow turning of a compass needle, almost imperceptible at first, but steady enough that one day you realize the direction has changed.

For many years I had lived inside the structures of the material world. Study, work, responsibility, family—these had been the equations I solved daily. They were complex problems, but problems nonetheless, and an engineer's instinct is always to find the solution.

But sometime in my forties, the equations began to feel incomplete.

Perhaps it was the bureaucracy of BHEL, where logic often lost to hierarchy. Perhaps it was the quiet fatigue of repeating the same technical conversations year after year. Or perhaps it was something deeper—a recognition that the material world, for all its complexity, could not answer the questions that had begun quietly surfacing inside me.

I found myself withdrawing.

Not from love, and not from responsibility entirely, but from the constant urgency that seemed to drive everything around me.

I spent more time at home. Writing. Reading. Sitting in silence.

Karma noticed the change first.

"You are turning inward," she said one evening while preparing tea.

I did not deny it.

It felt less like withdrawal and more like relocation—as if part of my life had quietly moved into another dimension, one that did not require the noise of the external world.

Strangely, I was content.

Sunita, meanwhile, moved in the opposite direction.

If my attention drifted toward the spiritual, hers remained firmly rooted in the material world.

Her career at Gandhi Medical College had begun gaining momentum. The research she had started years earlier was receiving recognition. Promotions followed slowly, but steadily.

She approached each stage with the same relentless discipline that had carried her through medical school and residency.

Where I began stepping away from the machinery of daily life, Sunita stepped further into it.

Bills. School forms. Hospital schedules. Professional conferences.

She managed it all with quiet efficiency.

In many ways, she became the anchor that kept the household functioning.

We never spoke about the contrast between us.

But it existed.

Two different ways of living inside the same house.

Karma remained the still point between us.

Her world had become increasingly spiritual, but unlike my withdrawal, hers did not remove her from the rhythm of family life.

She prayed every morning before sunrise. The sound of her voice reciting familiar Sanskrit verses drifted softly through the apartment before anyone else woke.

But after prayer, she returned immediately to the practical world.

Breakfast prepared. School uniforms ironed. Lunchboxes packed.

Her spirituality never separated her from life.

It deepened her presence inside it.

For Sarla and Karan, she became something more than a grandmother.

She became a bastion of unconditional love.

Children instinctively recognize love. And Karma offered it without conditions.

Sarla responded to it with quiet devotion.

Karan responded differently.

He challenged everything.

Karan's teachers often told us the same thing.

"He is extremely bright."

The statement was usually followed by another.

"But he does not apply himself consistently."

This puzzled many of them.

How could a child capable of solving complex problems lose interest halfway through simple assignments? How could someone who grasped concepts immediately become restless in classrooms that moved too slowly?

At home, the pattern continued.

Some evenings he buried himself in books for hours, completely absorbed. Other days he wandered outside before finishing even basic homework.

I watched him carefully.

There was something inside him that I recognized, though I could not name it.

Restlessness.

A refusal to follow predictable paths.

Sarla was different.

Whereas Karan zigzagged through life, as-if bouncing off of invisible boundaries, Sarla moved in straight lines. Disciplined. Focused. Responsible.

She had already decided to pursue medicine, following a path similar to her mother's.

In time she would enroll at Gandhi Medical College—the same institution where Sunita worked.

Her trajectory felt stable, understandable.

Karan's did not.

One journey during those years remains etched clearly in my memory.

Karan and I were traveling from Bhopal to Bombay on the Punjab Mail.

Train travel in India had its own rhythm. Vendors moved through compartments selling tea and snacks. Families shared food across narrow aisles. Conversations began easily between strangers.

Karan sat beside the window, watching the countryside blur past in long stretches of green and brown.

At one station a disabled boy, not much older than Karan, entered the compartment.

He moved by pushing himself forward with his arms in battered crutches, his legs folded beneath him in a way that suggested they had long ago stopped working.

Passengers glanced briefly and then returned to their newspapers.

He began asking for money.

Something about the boy caught my attention.

Perhaps it was the dignity with which he spoke, despite the humiliation of begging.

I gestured for him to come closer.

"What is your name?" I asked.

He seemed surprised.

"Rafiq," he replied.

We began talking.

At first he answered cautiously, perhaps expecting another passenger to dismiss him after a few polite questions. But as the conversation continued, his guard softened.

He told me where he had grown up. How an illness had taken away the use of his legs. How begging had become the only way he could survive.

Karan watched silently.

I asked him another question.

"If you could do something else," I said, "what would you choose?"

The man hesitated.

Then he said something simple.

"I would like to polish shoes."

He explained that many men at railway stations earned decent money shining shoes for travelers. It required little capital—only a box, polish, brushes.

But he had never been able to gather the money needed to begin.

The train continued rolling toward Bombay.

Our conversation continued with it.

By the time we approached Victoria Terminus in Bombay, an idea had already formed in my mind.

When the train stopped, Karan and I stepped onto the platform with our luggage.

Rafiq, on his crutches, followed us hesitantly.

Bombay in those days felt like another universe compared to Bhopal. The station itself was a world of movement—crowds flowing through arches, announcements echoing across platforms, vendors shouting over the noise.

We began walking through the station.

Karan looked confused.

"Where are we going?" he asked.

"Looking for something," I replied.

Eventually we found a small stall selling shoe polish kits — wooden boxes with brushes, polish tins, cloths.

I purchased one.

When I handed it to Rafiq, he looked at it for a moment as if he did not understand what it was.

Then the meaning reached him.

He did not speak.

Neither did I.

Some moments do not require words.

His eyes filled with tears.

Karan stood beside me, watching everything quietly.

Years later he would remember that moment in ways I could not have predicted.

But for me it was simple.

Sometimes helping someone stand does not require lifting them.

It requires giving them something they can stand upon.

During those years Karan gradually discovered something about himself.

He was good at studying.

Not in the disciplined way Sarla approached academics, but in bursts of intense focus that produced surprising results.

Examinations, especially, seemed to suit his mind.

The structure of problems, the logic of solutions—these gave direction to his restless energy.

By the time he reached his final years of school, the pattern became clear.

When darkness threatened to pull him inward, he turned to books.

Studying became more than preparation.

It became an escape.

In 1992 Karan sat for the Indian Institute of Technology (IIT) Joint Entrance Examination.

Across India, thousands of students prepared for that exam every year. For many families it represented not only academic opportunity but social mobility.

The results arrived weeks later.

Karan's All India Rank, 432.

The number fixed itself in my memory.

I had always hoped he might pursue electrical engineering, perhaps following the path I had walked decades earlier.

But Karan had his own ideas.

He chose Chemical Engineering at IIT Bombay.

The decision surprised me.

For a moment, I felt a small disappointment—the quiet hope of a father that his son might continue the same intellectual lineage.

But disappointment passes quickly when confronted with reality.

Children do not exist to fulfill the unfinished ambitions of their parents.

They arrive carrying their own equations.

I accepted his choice.

Radical acceptance, perhaps, though I would not have used those words then.

Three years before, Sarla's path became clearer.

She had already decided to pursue medicine and secured admission to Gandhi Medical College in Bhopal, the same institution where Sunita taught.

Where Karan's journey moved haphazardly through uncertainty before finding a direction, Sarla's remained steady.

Watching them both, I often thought about how siblings raised in the same house could become such different people.

Perhaps it was simply temperament.

Perhaps it was destiny.

Or perhaps the same household contains many different worlds.

By the early 1990s our household had settled into a delicate balance.

Sunita advanced steadily toward professorship, her professional reputation growing with each passing year.

Karma remained the emotional center of the family, offering the same quiet love she had given since the children were born.

Sarla studied medicine with the same discipline she had shown since childhood.

Karan prepared to leave for Bombay.

And I continued living between two worlds.

One foot still placed in the material responsibilities of work and family.

The other, drifting slowly toward a quieter, inward landscape where answers were not found in equations, but in silence.

Looking back now, I realize those years were not defined by conflict.

They were defined by tension.

The tension between the visible world and the invisible one.

Between ambition and acceptance.

Between the life we build and the life that quietly builds us in return.

At the time, however, I did not analyze it so carefully.

I simply lived.

And watched my children begin walking toward futures that would eventually carry them far beyond the small apartment where their story had begun.

CHAPTER 7
Leaving Home

Life rarely changes in a single moment. But sometimes a door closes quietly so another can open far away.

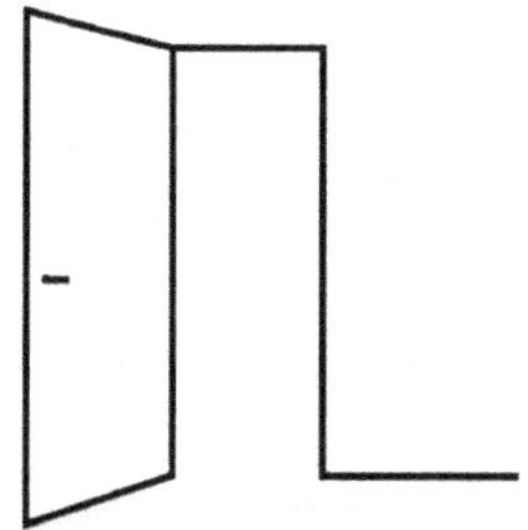

By the early 1990s, the work at BHEL had begun to exhaust me in ways that had nothing to do with engineering.

The technical problems remained interesting. Power systems were complex organisms, and the scale at which BHEL operated meant that every design decision had consequences far beyond the drawing board. That part of the work still held my attention.

But engineering was no longer the dominant force inside the institution.

Bureaucracy had grown thicker with every passing year. Layers of administration had multiplied. Decisions that once took days now required weeks of files moving between offices. And behind those layers operated another system entirely—one that no manual described but everyone seemed to understand.

Favors. Commissions. Quiet arrangements between suppliers and officials.

Most engineers learned to live with it. Some participated eagerly. Others simply ignored what they could not change.

I belonged to neither group.

There are certain lines that become visible only when you approach them. And once you see them clearly, you cannot pretend they do not exist.

The moment came one afternoon during a meeting with a supplier who had been bidding on a large contract.

His proposal contained several inconsistencies. The technical specifications did not align with the requirements of the system we were designing. When I pointed this out, he listened patiently, nodding at appropriate moments.

After the meeting ended, he lingered behind.

Then he placed a small envelope on the table between us.

"You will find this useful," he said quietly.

I did not open it.

Instead, I pushed it back across the table.

"I think you have misunderstood something," I said.

His smile faded slightly.

"Sir," he replied, lowering his voice, "everyone understands how these things work."

I stood up.

"Apparently I do not."

The conversation ended there.

Only later did I learn that the supplier was related by marriage to one of the senior executives inside the organization.

In retrospect, perhaps I should have anticipated what followed.

But engineers are trained to think in terms of cause and effect, not political consequence.

The first accusation arrived within weeks.

A complaint had been filed regarding procedural irregularities in a procurement decision I had made months earlier. An internal inquiry was opened. Files were requested. Meetings were scheduled.

At first I assumed the matter would resolve itself quickly.

After all, the records were clear.

But systems built to protect themselves do not operate according to logic.

They operate according to survival.

One investigation became another. Small administrative questions multiplied into formal reviews. Rumors circulated quietly through the corridors of the department.

Colleagues who had once spoken freely now became cautious.

The machinery of suspicion moved slowly but relentlessly.

For nearly two years, life inside BHEL became a kind of purgatory.

I attended meetings where accusations were implied but never fully stated. I responded to inquiries that seemed designed less to discover truth than to create uncertainty.

And gradually I realized something important.

The outcome had already been decided.

The system was not trying to determine whether I was right or wrong.

It was trying to restore equilibrium.

And the easiest way to restore equilibrium was to remove the person who had disrupted it.

The resolution arrived quietly.

One afternoon I was called into the office of a senior executive.

He spoke politely, even sympathetically.

"These situations," he said, "can become very complicated. For everyone involved."

He paused before continuing.

"There may be a more practical solution."

The solution he proposed was an early retirement.

The terms were generous by government standards. Pension benefits would remain intact. No formal findings would be recorded.

In effect, the institution would preserve its dignity, and I would regain my peace.

I listened carefully.

Strangely, I felt relief.

For years I had remained at BHEL out of responsibility—for family, for stability, for the predictable income that professional life required.

But by then another part of my life had already begun taking shape.

I had written ten textbooks on electrical engineering topics over the years. Three of them had been adopted into the national curriculum used by universities across India.

Royalty payments had begun arriving regularly.

Not enough to create wealth.

But enough to create freedom.

I accepted the offer.

When I walked out of the office that afternoon, I felt lighter than I had in years.

Leaving BHEL did not feel like an ending.

It felt like a return.

For the first time in decades I could devote myself fully to the activities that had always felt most natural to me—writing and teaching.

Students began visiting our home regularly. Some were young engineers preparing for competitive exams. Others simply wanted guidance in understanding difficult subjects.

I discovered that mentoring them brought a quiet satisfaction that corporate life had gradually eroded.

There was something deeply human about watching a young mind grasp a concept that had once seemed impossible.

Knowledge moving from one generation to the next.

Perhaps that had always been the work I was meant to do.

During those years Bhopal itself was changing.

The early 1990s were a volatile period across many parts of India. Political movements increasingly used religious identity as a tool of mobilization. In cities like Bhopal, where communities had lived side by side for generations, the rhetoric of division began seeping into everyday life.

Our neighborhood was predominantly Hindu.

Behind our house lived one Muslim family—quiet people who had been our neighbors for many years.

Karan happened to be home from IIT Bombay during one winter break when tensions in the city began rising.

Rumors spread quickly.

Clashes had occurred in other neighborhoods. Shops had been burned. Political leaders on both sides spoke publicly in ways that inflamed anger rather than calming it.

One evening, after dinner, we heard shouting in the distance.

Karan stepped outside onto the balcony.

A group of young men was moving down the street, shouting slogans and knocking on doors.

Karan turned toward me.

"They're looking for Muslim families," he said quietly.

I already knew.

Fear moves quickly through a neighborhood.

A few minutes later I heard a soft knock at the back door.

It was our neighbor.

His voice trembled slightly as he spoke.

"Sir," he said, "we were told it may not be safe tonight."

I did not hesitate.

"Bring your family inside," I said.

They entered quietly—husband, wife, two small children.

We turned off the lights and sat together in the living room.

Outside, the shouting continued for some time before gradually fading into the distance.

Karan sat beside me, saying nothing.

After a while he asked quietly, "Why are people doing this?"

I thought about the question for a moment.

"I do not know," I replied.

Then I added something else.

"But protecting someone who is afraid does not require understanding why others are angry."

The family stayed with us until morning.

When they returned to their house the next day, nothing more was said.

Some things do not require explanation.

They require only a decision.

Karan's life during those years unfolded far from Bhopal.

IIT Bombay was a world entirely different from the one he had grown up in.

The campus sat beside Powai Lake, surrounded by hills that softened the noise of the city beyond. Students from across India lived there together, united by the strange combination of competition and camaraderie that defined engineering education.

Karan seemed to thrive there.

Occasional phone calls arrived late at night. Letters appeared less frequently but contained long descriptions of hostel life, academic challenges, and the peculiar friendships that form when young people live together under pressure.

During his second year he developed severe abdominal pain.

The diagnosis was appendicitis.

Sunita traveled to Bombay immediately and stayed beside him during the surgery and recovery.

By the time I arrived a few days later, he was already beginning to recover.

I brought something with me.

My old Kinetic Honda scooter.

It had carried me through many years of commuting in Bhopal. The machine was aging, but it still ran reliably.

Karan's hostel friends gathered around it with interest.

They introduced themselves one by one—young men from different parts of India, speaking different languages but sharing the same intense curiosity about the world.

Watching them interact, I felt a quiet pride.

These were the people who would shape the future of the country.

Not politicians.

Students.

While Karan built his life in Bombay, Sarla continued her steady journey through medical school.

She excelled academically, earning respect from professors and classmates alike. The discipline she had shown since childhood had matured into professional competence.

In 1994 she completed her MBBS.

Soon afterward a proposal arrived.

The family of a young doctor from Sangli had expressed interest in marriage.

Arranged marriages often move quickly once both families agree.

Perhaps too quickly.

Karan objected strongly when he heard the news.

"She should have more time," he argued.

But the decision had already gathered momentum.

Sometimes families move forward because the structure of tradition makes stopping difficult.

Sarla accepted the match with quiet composure.

The wedding took place soon afterward.

Around the same time, another transition approached.

Karan began receiving fellowship offers from universities abroad.

The letters arrived one after another—institutions in the United States and Australia offering opportunities for graduate study in engineering.

He studied them carefully before making his decision.

The University of Wisconsin in Madison.

When he told us, I recognized the significance immediately.

This was no longer simply leaving home for Bombay.

This was leaving the country.

By then he had completed his degree at IIT Bombay among the top ten percent of his class.

The convocation ceremony took place in Bombay.

For reasons I cannot fully explain even now, Sunita and I did not attend.

Life sometimes moves quickly in ways that leave small regrets behind.

Karan never mentioned it.

But I remembered, later I found that he remembered as well.

By the time he prepared to leave for America, the household in Bhopal had already begun changing.

Sarla had started her married life.

Karan stood at the edge of another continent.

Sunita's career continued its upward trajectory.

Karma's health had begun declining slowly, though she rarely spoke about it.

And I had stepped away from the material machinery that had defined so much of my earlier life.

Looking back now, I realize that our family story was not defined by conflict or drama.

It was defined by departure.

Children leaving.

Structures shifting.

The quiet understanding that the house we had built together would no longer contain everyone who once lived inside it.

At the time, however, I did not think of it so clearly.

I simply watched my son prepare to cross an ocean.

And wondered what kind of man he would become once he arrived on the other side.

CHAPTER 8
Two Worlds

Life rarely divides cleanly between worlds. Yet sometimes we begin to live in two at once.

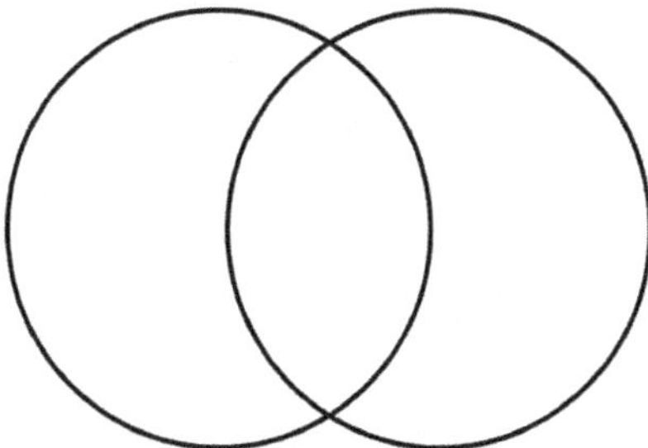

By the mid–1990s the house in Bhopal had begun to feel larger.

Not because its walls had changed, but because the people who once filled it were slowly leaving.

Sarla had married Naveen and moved to Sangli. Karan had crossed an ocean to begin his doctoral studies in America. The rooms that had once echoed with arguments about homework, laughter over meals, and the constant motion of young lives had grown quieter.

Only Karma's presence still filled the house completely.

She moved more slowly now. Age had begun to loosen its grip on her body, though her mind remained steady and alert. The rhythm of her days had not changed—morning prayers before sunrise, quiet conversations with neighbors, long hours spent in the kitchen preparing meals even when there were only a few of us left to eat them.

Watching her during those years, I began to understand something about devotion.

Karma had never spoken about sacrifice. She had simply lived it.

The departures had happened quickly.

First Sarla.

Her marriage to Naveen had taken her far from Bhopal, though Sangli was still within the geography of India. Naveen was a doctor—thoughtful, grounded, and deeply respectful toward our family. I had taken an immediate liking to him, though I rarely said so aloud.

Soon after their marriage, Sarla seemed to settle naturally into her new life.

Then came Karan's departure.

The day he left for the United States was strangely quiet. Airports have a way of compressing emotion into brief moments. Conversations become shorter than they should be. Questions remain unasked.

When his plane disappeared into the sky, I felt something shift inside me.

Parents spend years preparing children for independence.

But preparation does not soften the silence that follows.

After leaving BHEL, my life had gradually settled into a different rhythm.

Mornings began early. I spent several hours writing — refining manuscripts, responding to letters from publishers, revising chapters of textbooks that had begun circulating through universities across the country.

Students visited regularly.

Some arrived carrying thick notebooks filled with equations they could not solve. Others came simply to talk about their ambitions, their uncertainties, their hopes for the future.

Mentoring them brought a quiet satisfaction.

Knowledge moved easily between generations when both sides were willing to listen.

In the afternoons I worked in the garden.

Plants require patience. You cannot hurry their growth, only provide the conditions that allow it to occur naturally.

Perhaps that is true of people as well.

While my life became quieter, Sunita's grew busier.

Her academic career had entered a new phase. Years of research, teaching, and professional persistence had placed her firmly among the senior faculty at Gandhi Medical College.

Conferences. Committees. Research supervision.

Her days were filled with obligations that extended well beyond the hospital.

We rarely discussed the difference in our paths.

Perhaps we both understood it too clearly.

She lived fully inside the material world—the world of achievement, recognition, and measurable progress.

I had begun stepping away from it.

Yet our lives remained connected by the same household, the same memories, the same responsibilities that had shaped us for decades.

Sometimes marriages persist not because two people walk the same path, but because they accept that their paths will occasionally diverge.

One afternoon during those years, visitors arrived unexpectedly.

Karan's close friend from IIT Bombay—a young woman named Savita—had come to Bhopal with her parents. Their families had known each other through academic circles, and the visit seemed at first entirely social.

Tea was served. Conversations moved easily through the familiar subjects of education, careers, and family.

Then the purpose of their visit slowly emerged.

They wished to discuss a possible marriage between their daughter and Karan.

Arranged marriages in India often begin quietly, through conversations that unfold gradually across living rooms and dining tables.

Savita's parents spoke respectfully. They believed the two young people shared similar educational backgrounds and values.

I listened carefully.

When I later spoke to Karan on the telephone, I mentioned the proposal.

There was a long pause.

Then he declined.

Not rudely, not abruptly—simply with the quiet certainty of someone who already understood that his life had begun moving in another direction.

Paths sometimes diverge without conflict.

Particles moving through the same wave eventually separate.

In 1997 Sarla and Naveen welcomed their first child.

A girl.

They named her Adi.

When I first saw her, I felt something inside me soften in ways I had not expected. Infants carry a kind of light with them—a reminder that life continues its cycle regardless of the events surrounding it.

Adi's presence brought warmth to the house in Sangli.

Sarla seemed radiant in her new role as a mother. Naveen moved through the house with quiet attentiveness, balancing his medical responsibilities with the demands of a young family.

I began visiting Sangli more often.

During those visits, time moved differently.

Mornings began with the sound of Adi waking, her laughter echoing through the rooms. Evenings were spent walking through the neighborhood with Naveen, discussing medicine, philosophy, and the strange paths life sometimes takes.

Gradually I began building a house there.

Not out of necessity, but out of possibility.

Sangli carried a different energy from Bhopal—slower, more intimate, closer to the rhythm of ordinary life.

Being there brought me peace and joy.

Back in Bhopal, Karma's strength was beginning to fade.

Age moves quietly through the body at first. A small hesitation when standing. A longer pause between steps.

Eventually the signs become impossible to ignore.

She continued her daily prayers, though her voice had grown softer. The kitchen, once her domain, gradually shifted into the hands of others.

I spent more time sitting beside her in the evenings.

Sometimes we spoke.

More often we sat in silence.

One evening she looked at me and smiled faintly.

"You have always tried to understand life like a system," she said.

I laughed softly.

"That is what engineers do."

She nodded.

"But many things," she added, "cannot be solved that way."

Karma's final days were peaceful.

There was no sudden crisis, no dramatic moment of decline. Her body simply grew tired.

I stayed beside her constantly during those weeks.

Sunita visited when she could, though her responsibilities at GMC kept her away for long stretches.

Sarla came from Sangli.

Karan called frequently from America.

The distance in his voice was impossible to ignore.

Telephone lines carry sound clearly, but they cannot carry presence.

One evening I held the receiver while he spoke.

His voice broke.

On the other end of the line I could hear him sobbing.

Grief travels easily across oceans.

When the end came, it arrived quietly.

The house felt strangely calm, as if the air itself understood what had happened.

Later that day we carried Karma's body to the cremation ground.

Hindu rituals surrounding death are both simple and profound. They recognize that the body is only one part of existence—a temporary vessel returning to the elements from which it came. It was my responsibility to light the pyre.

The flames rose slowly.

I stood watching them without speaking.

I did not feel sadness in the way others expected.

Nor did I feel relief.

Instead there was a strange sense of alignment—as if something inside me understood that this moment belonged to a larger order of things.

The fire consumed the body that had carried Karma through nearly a century of life.

But the presence she had created—the love she had given so freely—remained everywhere.

In Sarla's patience.

In Karan's restless search for meaning.

In the quiet habits of the house she had shaped for so many years.

After her passing the remaining household felt different.

Not empty.

But rearranged.

Each of us seemed to move along our own trajectory—like charged particles responding to invisible forces.

Sarla raising her family in Sangli.

Karan pursuing knowledge across an ocean.

Sunita advancing steadily through the structures of academic medicine.

And I, increasingly aware that the boundary between the material and the spiritual worlds had begun drawing closer.

Karan returned home during the summer of 1998.

By then his life in America had already begun shaping him in ways I could only partially understand. His manner of speaking had changed slightly. His perspectives had widened.

We spent some time together during that visit.

But not as much as one might expect.

Distance has a way of creating invisible barriers even when two people sit in the same room.

Perhaps we both sensed it.

Perhaps we simply accepted it.

Some relationships evolve quietly over time, moving from closeness toward something more reflective.

Not absence.

But space.

Looking back now, those years between 1996 and 2000 marked a turning point in my life.

The structures that had once defined our household were dissolving.

The children had left.

My mother had passed.

Careers moved in different directions.

What remained was something simpler.

A garden.

A desk filled with manuscripts.

Students arriving at the door with questions about circuits and equations.

And the growing awareness that life, like any complex system, eventually moves toward equilibrium.

At the time I did not analyze it so carefully.

I simply watched the waves separate into individual particles.

And wondered where each of them would eventually land.

CHAPTER 9
The Quiet Distance

The distance between generations is not always separation. Sometimes it is simply space for each life to unfold.

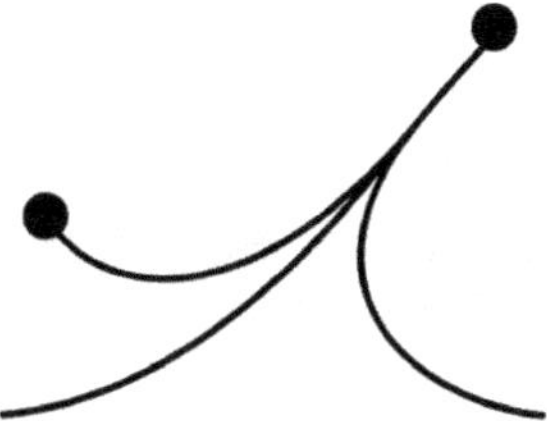

After Karma's passing, my life settled into a rhythm that felt both familiar and entirely new.

The house in Bhopal still stood as it always had—the same rooms, the same furniture, the same small garden that had slowly grown around it. But the center of gravity had shifted.

For decades Karma had been the silent force holding the household together. She had moved through life like a quiet current beneath the surface, carrying everything gently forward.

Without her presence, the structure of the family did not collapse.

But something inside it rearranged itself.

In the months that followed, I found myself spending more time alone.

Not out of loneliness.

Out of inclination.

My mornings began earlier than they once had.

Before sunrise I sat at my desk with a stack of books that had gradually begun occupying more of my attention.

The Upanishads.

The Vedas.

The teachings of Swami Vivekananda.

The writings of Ramakrishna Paramahansa.

These texts had existed for thousands of years, written by authors whose names were often lost to time. Yet the questions they asked felt strangely modern.

What is the nature of the self?

What does it mean to be alive?

Is consciousness something produced by the body, or something that merely passes through it?

As an engineer, I had spent most of my life studying systems.

Electrical systems behave according to predictable laws. Currents flow through circuits, energy moves through fields, and structures respond to forces.

But the deeper I read those ancient texts, the more I began recognizing a similar structure in human existence.

The body, they suggested, was not the fundamental unit of life.

The soul was.

The body was simply the vessel.

Temporary.

Useful.

But temporary.

If that were true, then much of what humans spend their lives pursuing begins to look different.

Wealth.

Status.

Recognition.

All of them matter deeply inside the material world.

But if the soul itself is eternal, then the time spent inside any one body becomes a brief passage through a much larger journey.

I did not claim to understand these ideas completely.

But they resonated with something inside me.

During those years I began spending more time in Sangli.

Sarla and Naveen had built a quiet life there, centered around their medical practice and the small rhythms of family life.

Little Adi had grown quickly.

Children change the atmosphere of a house in ways adults cannot replicate. Their curiosity moves freely through every room, transforming ordinary moments into discoveries.

When Adi laughed, the entire house seemed to brighten.

Watching Sarla raise her daughter, I sometimes saw reflections of Karma in her gestures—the same patient attention, the same instinct to care for others before thinking of herself.

Naveen welcomed my visits warmly.

In the evenings we often walked through the neighborhood discussing medicine, philosophy, and the strange ways human lives intersect.

Gradually the small house I had begun building there started to take shape.

Sangli felt closer to something I could not easily describe.

A slower rhythm.

A quieter energy.

And not far away was Belgaum.

Belgaum carried memories that stretched back to my earliest years.

It was there that Yadu still lived.

By the time I began visiting more frequently, he had grown old. His movements were slower, but his mind remained clear and generous as ever.

He had spent his life doing what he believed was right — mentoring students, helping families in need, supporting education wherever he could.

He never spoke about his contributions publicly.

Yet everyone in the town seemed to know his name.

When I visited him during those final months, our conversations were simple.

We spoke about the past.

About education.

About the unpredictable paths life sometimes takes.

One afternoon he looked at me and said something quietly.

“You always tried to understand the world with logic,” he said.

I smiled.

“That is what engineers do.”

He nodded.

“But remember,” he added, “logic is only one language the universe speaks.”

In early 2001 Yadu passed away.

There was no grand ceremony.

No elaborate announcement.

Yet on the day we gathered in Belgaum to remember him, nearly five hundred people appeared in the streets.

Students he had mentored.

Families he had helped.

Teachers whose work he had quietly supported.

Standing there beside Sunita, watching the crowd gather without invitation, I realized something profound.

Legacy is not built through recognition.

It is built through impact.

Around that time, Karan called one evening from Madison.

His voice sounded unusually deliberate.

"Can you both come on the speaker phone?" he asked.

Sunita and I sat beside each other while he spoke.

"I've met someone," he said.

There was a pause.

"She's a wonderful woman. I think I want to spend my life with her."

Her name was Diana.

He invited us to visit Madison and meet her family.

After the call ended, Sunita and I sat quietly for several minutes.

Parents spend years imagining how their children's lives will unfold. But those imaginations rarely survive contact with reality.

Finally Sunita spoke.

"Since he was ten years old," she said, "Karan has been the pilot of his own ship."

I looked at her.

"That is how I raised him," she continued. "To make his own decisions."

She paused before adding something else.

"I trust him."

I nodded.

So did I.

In the summer of 2001, Sunita and I traveled to Madison, Wisconsin.

The city surprised me immediately.

Lakes surrounded it on both sides, creating the impression that the entire place floated gently between water and sky. The university campus stretched across wide open spaces filled with students walking, reading, debating.

Karan was living in student housing on Harvey Street.

His roommate, Tran, greeted us warmly when we arrived. Tran was a history major, a second-generation Vietnamese American whose father had once been a general before fleeing Vietnam with his family.

At the time of our visit, Tran left for Los Angeles to see his family, leaving his room available for us.

We slept there during our stay.

The arrangement felt simple, unpretentious — exactly the kind of environment where young people shape their ideas about the world.

A few days later, Karan surprised us.

"I want to take you somewhere," he said.

We rented a Nissan Maxima and began driving west.

Diana joined us.

Hours passed as the landscape changed from farmland to open plains.

Eventually we reached the Black Hills of South Dakota.

It turned out our visit coincided with the Sturgis Motorcycle Rally.

Thousands of motorcycles filled the roads.

Leather jackets. Engines roaring. Music spilling out of roadside bars.

The scene felt chaotic and strangely joyful at the same time.

Karan explained why he had chosen the place.

"When I was little," he said, "you used to tell me stories about movies."

I laughed.

One film in particular had fascinated him—Alfred Hitchcock's North by Northwest.

The climactic scene of that movie takes place at Mount Rushmore. I had described the sequence vividly to him when he was a child.

Apparently the image had remained in his imagination.

"I wanted to bring you here," he said.

Something unexpected happened during that trip.

Walking through the Black Hills, I felt lighter than I had in years.

Perhaps it was the open landscape.

Perhaps it was the absence of responsibility.

Or perhaps it was simply being with my son in a place that existed outside the routines of our lives.

At one point we stopped along a trail overlooking the hills.

Motorcycles thundered along the distant roads.

Karan later told me that he saw something in me that day he had not seen in a long time.

Freedom.

The version of me he remembered from his childhood.

We talked, laughed, and walked for hours.

For a brief moment, time seemed to fold back on itself.

Later that week Diana took us to meet her family.

They lived on a farm outside the city.

The atmosphere there felt immediately genuine.

No ceremony. No performance.

Just people living their lives honestly.

Her mother greeted us warmly, guiding us through the house with a kindness that reminded me of someone I had known my entire life.

Karma.

Her father spoke quietly but thoughtfully about farming, history, and the strange ways communities form across generations.

In him I saw something of Yadu—the same calm wisdom that emerges from a life lived thoughtfully.

Sunita and I exchanged glances.

Without saying it directly, we both understood the same thing.

Karan had chosen well.

As we drove back toward Madison that evening, I leaned forward from the back seat.

"You are blessed, Karan," I whispered.

"Hold on to it."

One morning during that visit, Karan and I went for a walk together.

Madison was quiet at that hour. The lakes reflected the early sunlight, and students moved slowly across campus paths.

Our conversation wandered through many subjects.

Religion.

Science.

Philosophy.

The writings of Jiddu Krishnamurti.

Eventually we began discussing the nature of life itself.

I shared with him the ideas that had increasingly shaped my thinking.

"That which we call life," I said, "may simply be the soul learning through experience."

"The body is temporary," I continued. "A vessel the soul uses to understand existence."

Karan listened carefully.

Then he raised an objection.

"If that's true," he said, "then what about samadhi ? Saints who choose to leave the body voluntarily?"

He paused.

"That sounds like suicide."

I laughed.

"No," I said gently.

"Suicide is an escape."

"Samadhi is an embrace."

He considered this for a moment.

Finally he smiled.

"Maybe we should agree to disagree."

"Perhaps," I replied.

Some questions do not require immediate answers.

Before we left Madison, the wedding date was set.

June 15, 2002.

On the day of our departure, Karan and Diana drove us to O'Hare Airport in Chicago.

The highway stretched across miles of farmland as we talked about ordinary things—travel plans, family updates, small details that fill the spaces between larger decisions.

When we reached the terminal, we embraced briefly before walking toward the security gates.

As I turned back for one last look, I saw my son standing beside the woman he had chosen to share his life with.

For a moment I felt something very simple.

Gratitude.

Not for the life we had planned.

For the life that had unfolded.

And for the strange, beautiful way the universe sometimes brings distant paths together before sending them onward again.

CHAPTER 10

The Last Crossing

What we call death is only the moment when the traveler remembers that he was never the road.

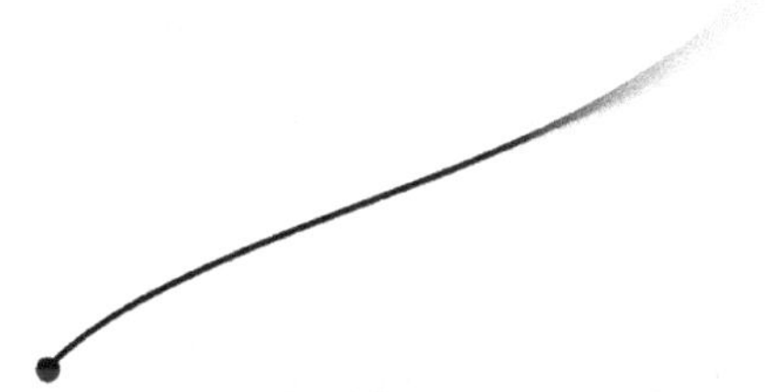

In the final year of my life, something inside me began changing in a way I had never experienced before.

For many years I had spoken about the spiritual world in abstract terms—ideas drawn from ancient texts, reflections shaped by observation, philosophical conclusions built slowly over time.

But during that period those ideas were no longer theoretical.

They became experience.

At first the moments appeared briefly. A sense of stillness during meditation. A quiet expansion of awareness during long walks. The sudden recognition that the boundaries between self and world were less rigid than they appeared.

Then the moments grew longer.

Hours sometimes passed in a state that is difficult to describe using ordinary language.

There was no effort involved.

No striving.

Only presence.

The Upanishads speak about oneness—the understanding that the individual self is not separate from the universal consciousness that animates all existence.

For most of my life that idea had seemed poetic but distant.

Now it felt obvious.

The divisions we perceive between people, between nature and consciousness, between life and death—all of them began to appear less like truths and more like temporary arrangements within a much larger system.

Joy appeared without cause.

Not excitement.

Not pleasure.

Something quieter.

Something deeper.

Simply being.

My life during that period moved gently between two places.

Sangli and Bhopal.

In Sangli the days unfolded slowly. Sarla and Naveen had created a home filled with warmth and stability. Little Adi filled the house with laughter and curiosity.

Children ask questions adults often stop asking.

"Why is the sky blue?"

"Where does the wind come from?"

"Why do people grow old?"

I sometimes wondered whether the spiritual traditions of the world were simply attempts to answer the same questions children ask naturally.

In Bhopal the routines remained familiar.

The garden.

My writing desk.

Students visiting with notebooks filled with equations.

Sunita continued her work at Gandhi Medical College with the same discipline that had defined her entire career.

Her days remained full.

Conferences.

Research supervision.

Departmental responsibilities.

Where my life had gradually moved inward, hers continued expanding outward.

We did not argue about these differences.

We simply lived alongside them.

In early 2002 Sunita began preparing for Karan's wedding.

Her approach was characteristically procedural.

Lists appeared on the dining table.

Travel plans.

Guest arrangements.

Ceremonial details.

Wedding traditions require organization, and organization had always been one of Sunita's strengths.

Yet beneath her efficiency I sensed something more complicated.

Excitement.

And something else.

A quiet sadness.

Parents recognize that certain events mark irreversible transitions. When a child marries, the center of their life moves permanently elsewhere.

One evening she looked up from her notes.

"You seem very calm about all this," she said.

I smiled.

"Time is a curious thing," I replied.

She looked at me skeptically.

"The past and the future are structures we use to organize experiences," I continued. "But the only moment that truly exists is the present."

She listened politely.

Whether she agreed with me I could not say.

Perhaps her own journey required different understandings.

In late May of 2002, we traveled to the United States.

Sunita.

Sarla.

Little Adi.

And I.

At O'Hare Airport, Karan greeted us with the same broad smile I remembered from his childhood.

He drove a 1990 Honda Civic LX, its engine humming steadily as we left Chicago behind and headed north toward Wisconsin.

The car was full.

Sunita and Sarla soon drifted into sleep after the long journey.

Adi asked occasional questions from the back seat.

Karan concentrated on the road.

I watched the landscape passing outside the window — farms stretching across the horizon, small towns appearing briefly before disappearing again.

Every so often I told a story or shared an observation.

The rhythm of travel settled around us.

Several hours later we arrived in Madison.

Karan and Diana lived in Eagle Heights, a cluster of university housing apartments perched on the western edge of campus.

The buildings were modest but surrounded by beauty.

Walking paths curved through green hills overlooking Lake Mendota. In the mornings sunlight shimmered across the water, and students walked quietly toward their laboratories or classrooms.

Diana greeted us at the apartment door.

The space was small.

A living room barely large enough to hold a few chairs, a narrow kitchen, bedrooms arranged along a short hallway.

But where there is love, space becomes irrelevant.

Laughter filled the rooms almost immediately.

The next few days unfolded with a rhythm that felt strangely perfect.

Karan and Diana left each morning for their respective graduate labs.

Sarla and Adi spent afternoons exploring nearby playgrounds.

Sunita occasionally joined Diana on errands across campus.

Karan and I walked together along the paths surrounding the lake.

The air carried the scent of water and early summer grass.

One night, sometime before midnight, the fire alarms began blaring.

The sound shattered the quiet of the apartment building.

Doors opened. Voices echoed through the hallway.

Diana reacted first.

She lifted Adi from the bed and hurried toward the exit.

Sarla and Karan followed.

Outside, residents gathered in the parking area while the alarms continued screaming.

Moments passed.

Then Karan must have noticed something.

Sunita and I were not there.

He turned immediately and ran back toward the building.

Halfway down the hallway he saw us emerging from the apartment.

Sunita moved slowly.

My arm rested around her shoulders for balance.

Something inside my body felt wrong.

My legs responded unevenly, as if the signals between mind and muscle had begun misfiring.

Karan reached us quickly.

Without speaking he slipped beneath my other arm.

Together we walked toward the exit.

By the time we reached the parking area the alarms had already stopped.

Apparently the system had tripped accidentally.

Residents began drifting back inside.

The emergency had passed.

Yet as we walked slowly toward the apartment again, I noticed the expressions around me.

Sunita looked worried.

Karan looked both concerned and agitated.

Sarla's face carried unmistakable anxiety.

And then Adi spoke.

"Why did the chicken cross the road?"

Everyone looked at her.

"To get away from the fire alarm!"

The tension dissolved instantly.

Children possess a remarkable ability to restore balance to situations adults take too seriously.

The following morning Karan insisted we visit a clinic.

I resisted at first.

But eventually I agreed.

We drove to an urgent care center near the university.

The doctors began asking questions about symptoms, medical history, medications.

Within minutes their expressions changed.

Nurses appeared quickly.

Machines were connected.

I remember being wheeled through bright corridors toward an intensive care unit.

The pace of activity increased dramatically.

Voices overlapped.

Instructions were given.

Monitors began displaying numbers I did not fully understand.

Despite the urgency surrounding me, I felt strangely calm.

Later that afternoon the first stroke occurred.

Then another.

Perhaps a third.

The doctors struggled to explain the sudden collapse of multiple systems.

My body, it seemed, had begun shutting down.

For five days I remained in the ICU.

Karan stayed beside the bed each night.

Sunita and Sarla moved between hospital corridors and waiting rooms.

Diana cared for Adi.

The medical staff did everything they could.

But some processes cannot be reversed.

One night, sometime before dawn, I became aware of Karan sitting beside me.

The room was dim.

Machines hummed quietly.

For a moment clarity returned.

I spoke softly.

"Thank you."

The words felt simple but carried many meanings.

Thank you for the life we had shared.

For the journey that had unfolded.

For the presence of family around me in that moment.

I remember telling him something else.

"That is all anyone can ask for."

Then the darkness returned.

By June 7th, the doctors spoke carefully with Sunita and Karan.

The probability of meaningful recovery was extremely small.

Even if consciousness returned, the damage to the brain would likely leave the body unable to function independently.

Life support machines could continue sustaining the body.

But the person who had once lived inside it might never return.

Sunita and Karan made the decision together.

Sometimes love requires letting go.

As the machines fell silent, something extraordinary happened.

The sensation was not physical.

It was not movement.

It was recognition.

The same presence I had glimpsed during meditation, during quiet moments of reflection, during the long walks of recent years — that presence now surrounded everything.

The boundaries that once defined my identity dissolved.

The body no longer felt central.

Instead there was a profound sense of belonging.

Not to a place.

To existence itself.

The universe did not feel distant.

It felt familiar.

Welcoming.

As if the journey through the human experience had simply reached its natural conclusion.

There was nothing left to achieve.

Nothing left to prove.

Nothing left to learn from the material world.

And nothing more the material world required from me.

The soul had completed its work inside that body.

What remained was continuation.

Not an ending.

A transition.

Into something that had always been present, waiting patiently beyond the boundaries of form.

CHAPTER 11

Witness

The witness was always present. Life was simply one place from which it looked.

The moment the machines fell silent, the body that had carried my name remained where it was.

But I was no longer inside it.

For most of my life I had believed that awareness belonged to the body—that the mind lived within the brain and that consciousness began and ended with the boundaries of skin.

That assumption dissolved immediately.

There was no sensation of leaving.

No movement through space.

The hospital room remained exactly as it had been moments earlier, quiet machines, dim light, the faint scent of antiseptic carried through conditioned air. The same people stood within it.

But the point from which the room was perceived had changed.

What had once been a single vantage point had widened.

Awareness remained, but it was no longer located within a body.

The form that had been called Sharan lay motionless on the bed. Nurses moved around it with practiced efficiency, removing lines, adjusting equipment, speaking softly in tones that carried both familiarity and respect. Hospitals learn to hold death without spectacle.

Near the bed stood Karan.

His posture was still, though not rigid. He looked at the machines for a moment before lowering his gaze toward the face that had once answered to the name "father."

Sunita stood a short distance away, close to the window. Her composure resembled the same professional calm she had carried throughout years inside medical institutions. Experience had trained her to stand inside moments like this without collapsing into them.

Sarla remained seated beside Diana. Their hands rested quietly together. In Diana's arms, Adi had fallen asleep, her breathing slow and even, untouched by the weight of the moment unfolding around her.

From the vantage that now encompassed the room, their responses appeared not as isolated emotions but as movements within a larger pattern.

Each person experienced the same event differently.

Karan's mind moved through questions that had no immediate answers.

Sunita held herself inside discipline, allowing procedure to guide the next necessary steps.

Sarla absorbed the moment quietly, the way she had always absorbed difficult things — through patience.

Diana protected the sleeping child without disturbing the fragile stillness that had settled over the room.

The event itself remained unchanged.

A body had ceased functioning.

But the meanings surrounding that event varied with each observer.

For a long time nothing moved except the ordinary rhythms of the hospital.

Eventually a nurse approached Karan and spoke gently. There were formalities that needed attention. Hospitals operate through systems, and even death must pass through their procedures.

Forms would be completed.

Doctors would speak with the family.

Arrangements would begin.

From the awareness of the witness that now observed without boundary, these actions did not appear trivial.

They were simply part of the continuity of life among the living.

The body that had once carried consciousness was now an object within that continuity.

Outside the hospital building, the city continued without interruption.

Cars moved through the streets of Madison.

Students crossed the paths of the university campus beside Lake Mendota.

Laboratories remained lit with the quiet work of people pursuing questions about chemistry, physics, medicine, and countless other disciplines.

Human activity rarely pauses for the passing of a single life.

From the wider perspective now present, those countless movements appeared interconnected in ways that had once been invisible.

Lives unfolded along trajectories shaped by choices, circumstances, and influences that extended far beyond individual awareness.

Karan remained beside the bed longer than the others.

Eventually Sunita approached him and placed a hand gently on his arm. The gesture was small but carried meaning that required no words. Together they stepped away from the bed and followed the nurse toward the hallway.

The body remained where it was.

But what had once animated it was no longer confined to that form.

The ancient texts had often spoken of the witness—the awareness that observes experience without becoming limited by it.

For many years I had considered those passages intellectually.

Now the meaning revealed itself directly.

The witness had always been present.

Human life had simply provided one vantage point from which to observe.

From this new state of awareness, moments from different periods of that life did not appear as distant memories.

They existed simultaneously.

Conversations with students in the garden in Bhopal.

Evenings in Sangli watching Adi take uncertain steps across the courtyard.

The long drive through the Black Hills with Karan, Diana, and Sunita as motorcycles filled the highways.

Each moment existed within the larger field of awareness like patterns within a current.

Time no longer moved in a straight line.

It resembled a landscape in which many points remained visible at once.

Human perception organizes life sequentially.

But the structure of experience itself was far less rigid.

As the family walked slowly down the hospital corridor, their footsteps fading into the ordinary sounds of the building, another understanding began to settle into clarity.

The life that had ended inside that room was only one expression within a much larger system.

Its influences would continue unfolding through the lives that remained.

Karan would carry questions that would shape his thinking for years.

Sunita would return to the world of medicine, though something inside her understanding had shifted quietly.

Sarla would return to Sangli, raising her daughter inside the rhythms of family life.

Diana, newly connected to the family, would become part of the continuing story that none of them could fully predict.

From the perspective of the witness, these developments appeared not as separate events but as evolving patterns.

Human lives often appear random when viewed from within them.

From a wider field of awareness of the witness, patterns emerge.

Not rigid plans.

Not predetermined outcomes.

But currents that guide experience toward forms of learning and understanding.

The form called Sharan had completed its role inside that process.

The awareness that had once experienced life through that body now remained free of its limitations.

There was nothing to accomplish.

Nothing to correct.

Only observation.

The living would continue their journeys through time.

And the witness would remain present—not as a person, but as awareness itself—watching the unfolding patterns of existence without the boundaries that had once defined a single human life.

CHAPTER 12
Rituals of the Living

A ceremony does not change what has happened. It changes how the living carry it.

When the family left the hospital, the body remained behind.

From the perspective of the living, this separation carried weight. Hospitals operate through clear boundaries. The living depart. The dead remain within institutional care until arrangements are completed.

From the perspective of the witness, the distinction appeared procedural rather than existential.

The form that had once been called Sharan rested quietly within the building, now subject to the orderly processes that modern societies apply to death.

Outside, the world continued moving.

The parking lot lights glowed against the late evening sky. Cars entered and exited the hospital grounds with the same steady rhythm they had followed earlier that day. Somewhere inside the building a child was being born. Somewhere else another family waited anxiously beside a different hospital bed.

Human institutions hold life and death within the same walls.

Karan drove the family back toward the apartment in Eagle Heights.

The car moved through familiar streets near the university campus. Streetlights passed in steady intervals along the road. The lakes that surrounded the city lay dark and quiet beneath the night sky.

Inside the car very little was said.

Silence is not always emptiness. Sometimes it is the most stable form of communication available.

Adi slept beside Sarla in the back seat. Diana sat beside her, watching the child carefully as the car moved through intersections and traffic lights. Sunita looked forward through the windshield, her posture composed, her attention already moving toward the tasks that would follow.

Karan kept both hands on the steering wheel.

His mind moved through practical questions.

Who should be contacted first.

What arrangements needed to be made.

Which institutions would require documentation.

Human grief often begins by organizing itself into action.

The following morning the work began.

Telephone calls were placed across time zones. Relatives in India received the news with voices that carried both shock and recognition. Death, though inevitable, always arrives with the force of interruption.

Colleagues from the university contacted Karan throughout the day. Some offered assistance with logistical arrangements. Others spoke briefly, unsure what words were appropriate within such moments.

Sunita spoke with hospital administrators and funeral service coordinators. Her voice remained steady, moving through the necessary details with the same clarity she had used throughout her medical career.

Documentation.

Transport arrangements.

Legal confirmations.

The language surrounding death in modern institutions is precise. Each step must be recorded, authorized, and verified.

From the perspective of awareness, these procedures appeared neither cold nor impersonal.

They represented society's effort to bring order to an event that resists understanding.

Later that afternoon the family returned briefly to the hospital.

The building appeared unchanged. Nurses moved through corridors. Doctors spoke with patients. Elevators opened and closed with the same mechanical rhythm.

Inside the room, the body had been prepared.

The lines and monitors were gone. The form lay covered beneath a simple white sheet, the face visible, the features calm in a way that resembled sleep.

The living approached carefully.

Karan stood beside the bed again. His gaze remained fixed on the still face for a long time.

Sunita placed her hand lightly on the edge of the mattress. The gesture contained no outward display of emotion, but its meaning was unmistakable.

Sarla spoke quietly to Diana while Adi remained outside the room with a nurse who had volunteered to sit with her.

Ritual begins long before formal ceremonies.

It begins with gestures.

With moments of stillness.

With the recognition that something permanent has occurred.

Later, discussions turned toward the question of what should follow.

The family carried cultural traditions that had developed thousands of years earlier, far from the city where they now stood.

In India, death is accompanied by ceremonies that acknowledge the body's return to the elements—fire, air, water, earth.

Here in Wisconsin, those traditions would need to adapt to a different landscape, a different legal structure, a different set of institutional processes.

Karan and Sunita spoke quietly with the funeral director.

Options were explained.

Cremation.

Transportation.

Memorial services.

Documentation required for international communication.

The director spoke carefully, accustomed to guiding families through decisions that felt unfamiliar and overwhelming.

From the perspective of the witness, these conversations reflected something fundamental about human societies.

Ritual does not exist for the dead.

It exists for the living.

Through ceremony, people organize their grief into forms that can be shared.

They transform private loss into communal acknowledgment.

In doing so, they create continuity between past and future.

Later that evening the family gathered in the small apartment at Eagle Heights.

The rooms were quiet.

Diana prepared tea for everyone. Sarla sat beside Adi, explaining gently that her grandfather would not be returning home.

Children understand loss differently than adults. Their questions are direct, unburdened by the abstractions that complicate adult thought.

"Where did he go?" Adi asked.

Sarla paused before answering.

"He has become part of the universe," she said softly.

The child considered this for a moment before nodding, satisfied for now with an explanation that left room for imagination.

In the days that followed, messages continued arriving.

Former students wrote letters describing how their careers had been shaped by guidance offered many years earlier. Academic colleagues shared memories of conversations that had extended late into the night during conferences and research collaborations.

Friends from Bhopal and Sangli called to speak with Sarla and Sunita, their voices carrying echoes of shared history.

Each message revealed another thread connecting the life that had ended to the lives that continued.

From within human experience, these expressions appear as individual memories.

From the wider field of awareness, they resembled the unfolding of a network.

Influence travels through time in ways the individual rarely perceives.

A teacher's words spoken decades earlier may guide a student's decision years later.

A gesture of kindness may ripple quietly through families and communities long after the moment itself has passed.

The form called Sharan had ended.

But the patterns it helped create remained active.

One evening Karan stepped outside the apartment alone.

The sky above Madison was clear. The lights of the campus reflected faintly against the surface of Lake Mendota.

He stood there for several minutes without moving.

Human beings often search for meaning during such moments. They ask questions about fairness, purpose, and destiny.

From the wider perspective now present, those questions appeared as part of the natural process through which consciousness examines itself.

Eventually Karan returned inside.

The living continued organizing the days ahead.

Phone calls would be made.

Ceremonies would be planned.

Travel arrangements would unfold across continents.

Life would move forward, carrying memory with it.

And the witness remained present—not within any single body, not within any single moment—observing the quiet rituals through which human beings transform loss into continuity.

CHAPTER 13

Continuation

Life does not replace what has been lost. It learns to continue beside it.

In the days that followed, the rhythms of the living began to reorganize themselves.

Human lives rarely pause for long. Even the most profound interruptions gradually become part of the ongoing structure of daily existence. Responsibilities remain. Decisions require attention. The future continues advancing regardless of the past.

From within that wider awareness of the witness, these adjustments appeared not as emotional responses but as the natural stabilization of a system after disturbance.

The apartment at Eagle Heights became the center of those adjustments.

The rooms were small but functional. Books and papers still occupied the desk where Karan had been working before the hospital visit. Diana's research materials remained neatly arranged near the dining table. The ordinary artifacts of graduate student life—notebooks, journals, stacks of printed articles—continued to occupy their familiar spaces.

Life does not remove these objects when death occurs.

They remain where they were, quietly reminding the living that their own journeys continue.

Karan moved through the apartment with a careful deliberation. Telephone calls occupied much of his time. Conversations with family members in India extended late into the night as the differences in time zones created windows of communication across continents.

Relatives in Bhopal and Sangli absorbed the news with the same mixture of grief and acceptance that accompanies the passing of an elder. Voices carried memories across the telephone lines—stories from decades earlier, fragments of shared history that suddenly felt more significant than they had before.

From the perspective of awareness, those conversations revealed something subtle.

Human memory does not preserve life in chronological order.

Instead it gathers moments that carry meaning.

A gesture offered many years earlier.

A piece of advice remembered unexpectedly.

A quiet kindness that had seemed ordinary at the time.

These fragments formed the narrative through which the living now understood the life that had ended.

Sunita continued managing the practical arrangements that followed death.

Forms needed to be completed. Legal procedures required confirmation. Conversations with funeral services and hospital administrators continued throughout the day. Her voice remained steady, focused on the clarity of each task rather than the emotional weight surrounding it.

Discipline had always been her method of maintaining balance.

From the perspective of the witness, this response appeared neither avoidance nor suppression.

It was simply the structure through which her mind processed disruption.

Sarla moved more gently through the apartment.

Much of her attention centered on Adi.

Children recognize changes in the emotional atmosphere around them even when the details remain unclear. Sarla spoke to her daughter with quiet patience, answering questions simply, allowing the child's curiosity to guide the conversation rather than imposing explanations that belonged to the adult world.

Adi accepted the new reality in the direct way children often do.

She asked where her grandfather had gone.

She listened carefully to the answers offered.

Then her attention returned to the small discoveries that filled her days—the playground near the lake, the ducks that moved across the water at sunset, the unfamiliar sounds of the campus buses that passed along the roads near Eagle Heights.

From the vantage of awareness of the witness, her response illustrated something fundamental.

Human life continues most visibly through the young.

Where adults see endings, children perceive only change.

One afternoon Karan and Diana walked together along the paths beside Lake Mendota.

The early summer air carried the scent of water and newly cut grass. Students moved along the trails with backpacks and bicycles, their conversations drifting through the quiet spaces between trees.

Karan spoke occasionally, though long intervals of silence passed between sentences. Diana listened without interrupting.

From the wider field of awareness of the witness, the interaction appeared balanced.

Not an attempt to resolve grief.

Simply the presence of two lives moving forward together.

Human relationships often reveal their strength during periods of uncertainty.

The influence of one life upon another rarely ends when physical presence disappears.

Instead it continues through decisions, questions, and habits of thought that shape the paths people follow.

Later that evening Karan returned to his desk.

The research problems that had occupied his attention before the hospital visit remained unresolved. Equations still covered the pages of his notebooks. Data sets waited to be analyzed.

For a long time he sat quietly without opening the notebook.

Eventually he began working again.

From within human experience, this return to ordinary tasks might appear abrupt.

From the perspective of awareness of the witness, it reflected something deeper.

Human beings carry their losses forward while continuing to participate in life.

Work resumes.

Conversations continue.

The structure of daily existence absorbs disruption and slowly reestablishes equilibrium.

Sunita spent part of the following day speaking with Sarla about travel arrangements.

There were decisions to be made regarding the ceremonies that would follow. Cultural traditions carried expectations that extended across oceans. Family members in India expressed their wishes through long conversations that moved between grief and practicality.

The discussions remained calm.

Each person understood that distance required adaptation.

Traditions that had once been performed within ancestral homes would now unfold across continents.

From the perspective of the witness, these negotiations revealed another pattern within human societies.

Customs endure because they evolve.

Even the most ancient rituals adapt themselves to new circumstances while preserving the meaning that originally shaped them.

One evening the family gathered again in the small living room.

Tea was poured. Conversation moved quietly between subjects — travel plans, messages received from relatives, small details that helped organize the days ahead.

Adi sat on the floor drawing pictures on a sheet of paper.

After a few minutes she held the drawing up for the others to see.

It showed a simple figure standing beside a large circle representing the sun.

"That's Ajoba (a term of endearment for grandfather in Marathi)," she said.

No one corrected her.

Children often express understanding through symbols rather than explanation.

From the vantage of awareness of the witness, the drawing resembled something deeper than the child intended.

Human beings often imagine that those who have died move somewhere distant.

Yet the patterns of influence they create remain woven into the lives that continue.

The figure in the drawing did not represent a location.

It represented continuity.

Outside the apartment the campus lights reflected softly across the surface of the lake.

The city continued its quiet movements.

Within the apartment the living prepared themselves for the ceremonies and decisions that would follow in the coming days.

And the witness remained present—observing the gradual reorganization of human lives after the passing of one who had once stood among them, watching as influence moved quietly forward through the generations that continued the journey.

CHAPTER 14
Propagation

Like a wave across water, a life continues long after its center disappears.

Human lives appear linear from within them.

Days follow nights. Years accumulate quietly behind birthdays, graduations, illnesses, celebrations. Memory organizes these events into stories that create the impression of sequence.

From the wider field of awareness, the structure of time reveals itself differently.

Moments do not disappear.

They remain present within the larger field of experience, like currents within a vast body of water. What human perception calls the past continues influencing the movement of everything that follows.

After the days of ritual and adjustment in Madison, the lives that had briefly converged in Eagle Heights began to separate again.

The wedding date approached.

June moved steadily forward across the calendar.

Preparations unfolded quietly within the small apartment near Lake Mendota. Lists appeared on tables. Conversations with relatives crossed continents through telephones and letters. Diana and Karan continued their research work during the day, returning in the evenings to discussions about travel, ceremonies, and the arrival of family members.

From within human perception, the absence of a father at a wedding carries weight.

From the perspective of the witness, absence becomes another form of presence.

Influence does not depend on physical proximity.

The patterns that shape human decisions often originate years earlier, in conversations, examples, and questions that continue echoing through the mind long after the person who spoke them is gone.

On the morning of the wedding, sunlight moved across the buildings of the university campus.

Guests gathered.

Families met for the first time.

Ceremonies unfolded according to traditions that blended cultures separated by geography but united through intention.

Karan stood beside Diana as vows were exchanged.

From the perspective of the witness, the moment represented not a beginning but a continuation.

Two lives were aligning their trajectories.

Their decisions would influence events that neither of them could yet imagine.

After the ceremony the families gradually dispersed.

Sunita returned to India.

Sarla and Naveen resumed their medical work in Sangli, where Adi continued growing within the steady rhythms of family life.

Madison returned to its familiar academic pace.

Students arrived and departed with each new semester. Laboratories resumed their quiet cycles of experimentation and analysis.

Within that environment Karan completed the final stages of his doctoral work.

The process required concentration that often extended late into the night. Pages of calculations accumulated across his desk. Data sets expanded into notebooks filled with annotations and corrections.

From the vantage of awareness, these efforts represented more than professional advancement.

Human beings often believe they pursue knowledge for practical reasons — careers, recognition, achievement.

Yet beneath those motivations lies something deeper.

Curiosity.

The same impulse that drives a child to ask questions about the sky eventually guides adults toward scientific inquiry, philosophy, and exploration.

Karan's work reflected that impulse.

Equations written across paper represented attempts to understand the structures governing the material world.

Yet the questions that moved quietly beneath those calculations extended further.

What patterns govern existence?

Why does order emerge from apparent chaos?

Where does consciousness arise within systems of matter and energy?

The mind that had once listened to stories beside a small garden in Bhopal continued asking the same questions.

Time moved forward.

Degrees were completed.

New responsibilities appeared.

Karan and Diana began constructing the next stage of their lives together, balancing professional commitments with the practical realities of building a household in a foreign country.

From within the wider awareness, their partnership revealed something fundamental about human relationships.

Two individuals rarely travel identical paths.

Yet when their trajectories align with mutual respect and non judgemental curiosity, they create a system capable of sustaining both stability and growth.

Across the ocean, Sunita returned to the routines of Gandhi Medical College.

Lectures resumed.

Students arrived with questions about anatomy, physiology, and clinical practice. Research meetings filled her calendar. Conferences and administrative responsibilities occupied the hours that extended beyond the classroom.

Her life continued operating within structures she understood well.

Discipline.

Organization.

Responsibility.

From the perspective of awareness, her response to loss remained consistent with the patterns that had shaped her character for decades.

Human beings often stabilize themselves by returning to environments where their roles remain clearly defined.

The hospital and the classroom provided that structure.

In Sangli, Sarla and Naveen continued building their medical practice.

Patients arrived each day carrying concerns that ranged from minor illnesses to life-altering diagnoses. The routines of medicine require attention that rarely allows extended reflection.

Within their home, Adi moved steadily from childhood toward adolescence.

Curiosity expanded.

Questions multiplied.

Her drawings gradually evolved from simple figures toward scenes that captured the small details of daily life — houses, trees, people standing together beneath wide skies.

From the field of awareness, these developments formed patterns repeating across generations.

Every human life begins within the protective structures created by others.

Gradually those structures expand outward as each generation begins shaping the environment for those who follow.

Influence propagates quietly.

Not through dramatic declarations.

Through daily habits.

Through the values communicated in ordinary conversations.

Through examples that children observe long before they fully understand them.

Years passed.

Seasons cycled across continents.

Madison experienced winters that covered the campus in deep snow and summers when the lakes filled with sunlight and movement.

Sangli moved through monsoon rains and dry seasons that shaped the rhythms of agriculture and village life.

Bhopal continued its steady expansion as new neighborhoods appeared around the older sections of the city.

Human perception experiences these changes as the passage of time.

From the wider field of awareness, they resembled the unfolding of patterns within a living system.

Events described as separate — a graduation, a new research project, a child entering school — existed as interconnected developments within the same field of influence.

The life that had once been called Sharan had ended.

Yet the currents it helped shape continued moving through the lives that followed.

Karan occasionally remembered conversations from years earlier.

A remark about systems and equilibrium.

An observation about the nature of time.

A story about a film that had once inspired a childhood imagination.

These recollections appeared randomly within his thoughts, emerging during moments of reflection or during long walks beside the lakes of Madison.

From within human experience such memories seem spontaneous.

From the perspective of awareness, they represent the persistence of influence.

Ideas propagate through consciousness in much the same way that energy propagates through physical systems.

They move quietly, shaping perception long after their origin is forgotten.

The witness remained present throughout these years.

Not intervening.

Not directing events.

Simply observing the propagation of patterns through human lives that continued unfolding across continents and generations.

And gradually another realization began forming within that awareness.

The influence of one life does not travel only through family.

It travels through every mind it has touched.

Students who had once visited a quiet house in Bhopal carried fragments of earlier conversations into their own classrooms and laboratories.

Colleagues remembered questions that had reshaped their thinking during late discussions at conferences.

Friends carried forward gestures of kindness that had seemed small at the time.

Human lives rarely perceive the full extent of their influence.

But from the perspective of the witness, the propagation of those influences appeared unmistakable.

Like waves moving outward across the surface of water long after the original stone has disappeared beneath it.

CHAPTER 15
Inheritance

The most enduring inheritance is not wealth or name, but the questions we teach others to keep asking

As the years continued unfolding, the lives that had once converged briefly in Madison moved outward along their separate trajectories.

From within human perception, these developments appeared gradual.

Careers advanced.

Homes were established.

Responsibilities expanded.

The movement resembled the unfolding of a larger structure—a network of influences spreading through time, each decision altering the direction of the next.

Karan and Diana entered the next phase of their lives with the quiet determination that had already characterized their partnership.

The academic world in which they had been trained continued demanding long hours of concentration. Research problems rarely yield easily. Solutions require patience, revision, and the willingness to accept uncertainty for extended periods.

The work that had once occupied Karan's desk in a small apartment overlooking Lake Mendota gradually expanded into larger professional responsibilities.

Projects grew in complexity.

Collaborations extended across institutions.

Students arrived seeking guidance in the same way he had once sought guidance from those who came before him.

From within that wider awareness of the witness, these developments revealed a familiar pattern.

Knowledge rarely moves in isolation.

It travels through mentorship.

Ideas pass from one mind to another, evolving as they move through different contexts and experiences.

The student becomes the teacher.

The question becomes the method.

The method becomes the foundation for further inquiry.

Diana's own work evolved alongside these developments.

Their partnership remained grounded in the same quiet equilibrium that had first appeared during the long walks beside Lake Mendota years earlier.

Human relationships, when sustained over time, reveal a rhythm similar to the systems studied by scientists.

Periods of expansion.

Moments of tension.

Adjustments that restore balance.

Through these cycles, stability emerges not from rigidity but from adaptability.

Across the ocean, Sunita's life continued within the familiar structures of Gandhi Medical College.

Years of teaching had placed her in positions of increasing responsibility within the institution. Students arrived each year carrying the same mixture of ambition and uncertainty that had characterized earlier generations.

Lectures continued.

Clinical supervision filled long hours within hospital wards.

Administrative meetings extended into evenings that once might have been spent quietly at home.

From the perspective of awareness, her path demonstrated a principle that appears repeatedly within human societies.

Purpose often reveals itself through service to systems larger than the individual.

The hospital functioned as one such system.

Thousands of patients moved through its corridors each year.

Doctors, nurses, and students worked within its structures to restore health where possible and provide care where restoration proved impossible.

Within those routines Sunita maintained the discipline that had guided her throughout life.

Her days remained organized around responsibilities rather than reflection.

Yet influence moved quietly through her work.

Students who passed through her lectures carried fragments of her instruction into hospitals across the country.

From within human perception such influence appears limited.

From the wider field of awareness of the witness, it formed part of a much larger propagation.

In Sangli, Sarla and Naveen's medical practice expanded steadily.

Their days began early and ended late, shaped by the needs of the patients who arrived at their clinic seeking relief from illness and uncertainty.

Medicine places its practitioners in direct contact with the fragility of human life.

Birth and death, recovery and decline, hope and disappointment appear within the same day.

Through those experiences, physicians learn a form of patience that cannot be taught in classrooms.

Adi continued growing within this environment.

The child who had once drawn simple figures beside the sun gradually entered adolescence. School introduced her to subjects that expanded her curiosity beyond the boundaries of the household.

Mathematics.

Literature.

History.

The questions that once filled her drawings began appearing within notebooks and conversations at the dinner table.

From the vantage of witness, these developments echoed patterns that had appeared earlier within the family.

Curiosity propagates.

The intellectual inheritance that had moved from one generation to another continued expressing itself in new forms.

Meanwhile, the wider world continued its own movements.

Cities expanded.

Technologies evolved.

Communication between continents became increasingly immediate as digital networks replaced the slower systems of earlier decades.

From within human experience these changes often appear revolutionary.

From the perspective of awareness of the witness, they resemble another phase in the long process through which human societies organize information and connection.

Karan's work increasingly intersected with these expanding networks.

Research collaborations formed across geographical boundaries. Ideas exchanged through digital communication moved rapidly between laboratories separated by thousands of miles.

The scale of inquiry expanded.

Problems once confined to individual research groups now involved teams distributed across institutions and countries.

Yet beneath these developments the deeper pattern remained unchanged.

Human curiosity continued seeking understanding.

The same questions that had once occupied philosophers beneath oil lamps and scientists beside early mechanical instruments persisted within modern laboratories illuminated by computer screens.

What governs the behavior of matter?

What principles organize complex systems?

Where does consciousness arise within the structures of the universe?

These questions remained present within Karan's work, though they often appeared indirectly within the language of equations and experiments.

Occasionally, during quiet moments between responsibilities, memories surfaced unexpectedly.

A remark once spoken during a conversation in Bhopal.

An observation about equilibrium within complex systems.

A reflection about time as a structure created by perception.

Such thoughts did not arrive as instructions.

They appeared as fragments of earlier influence moving quietly through the mind.

From the wider field of awareness of the witness, these moments represented the continuation of intellectual lineage.

Ideas do not vanish when their originators disappear.

They persist within the minds they have shaped.

Years continued moving forward.

Families expanded.

Students graduated and moved into their own professional paths.

Cities changed gradually around the people who lived within them.

Through all of these developments the witness remained present.

Not guiding.

Not correcting.

Simply observing.

And within that observation another realization emerged with increasing clarity.

Human beings often imagine inheritance primarily in biological terms.

Parents pass genetic material to children.

Families share physical traits across generations.

Yet another form of inheritance travels alongside biology.

Intellectual inheritance.

Ethical inheritance.

Questions passed forward through conversation and examples.

The life once called Sharan had contributed to that inheritance in ways that extended beyond immediate family.

Students who had once visited a modest house in Bhopal carried fragments of earlier conversations into their own careers.

Colleagues remembered discussions that had shifted their thinking during moments that seemed ordinary at the time.

Children who had grown up hearing certain questions repeated around the dinner table continued asking those questions as adults.

These influences resembled patterns propagating through a vast system.

No single life directs the system.

Yet each life contributes energy to its movement, and is entangled with the whole, like a propagating wave.

The witness observed these currents moving steadily forward through time.

And gradually the distinction between individual lives and the larger system they formed began to appear less definite.

What humans call a life may simply be a temporary concentration of influence within a much wider field of experience.

The patterns continue long after the individual form dissolves.

Just as waves continue moving across water long after the stone that created them has disappeared beneath the surface.

CHAPTER 16
Convergence

Every search for understanding eventually discovers the searcher within it.

As the second decade of the century unfolded, the currents that had once diverged across continents began slowly moving toward new intersections.

From within human perception, these developments appeared unrelated.

Career decisions.

Unexpected challenges.

Moments of reflection triggered by circumstances that seemed accidental.

Yet from the wider field of awareness of the witness, the movements resembled the gradual convergence of trajectories that had been evolving for decades.

Karan's professional life continued expanding in scope and responsibility.

The questions that had once occupied a graduate student's notebooks now appeared within larger frameworks of inquiry—collaborations involving researchers, institutions, and technologies capable of exploring problems at scales unimaginable a generation earlier.

Computational systems analyzed patterns within enormous data sets.

Laboratories connected through global networks exchanged information continuously.

Scientific understanding advanced through the coordinated efforts of thousands of minds.

From the perspective of the witness, these developments illustrated a transformation occurring quietly across human civilization.

Knowledge itself had begun functioning as a distributed system.

No single individual possessed a complete understanding of the structures being explored.

Instead, fragments of insight moved between minds, assembling themselves gradually into larger patterns of comprehension.

Yet even within these vast networks, the experience of inquiry remained deeply personal.

Late evenings still found Karan sitting alone at a desk, examining equations or reviewing experimental results while searching for clarity within complex systems.

During those moments the mind occasionally returned to questions that had appeared long before the language of research proposals and institutional responsibilities entered his life.

Questions about order.

Questions about causality.

Questions about the nature of awareness itself.

The mind often encounters such questions indirectly, through disciplines that appear unrelated.

Mathematics.

Physics.

Chemistry.

Biology.

Philosophy.

Each attempts to describe patterns within reality using its own language.

Yet beneath these different vocabularies lies a shared curiosity.

What is the nature of existence?

How do individual elements organize themselves into complex systems?

Why does consciousness arise within matter capable of reflecting upon itself?

These questions had once appeared during conversations beside a small garden in Bhopal.

Now they emerged again, quietly, within a different context.

Across the ocean, Sunita's life gradually moved toward a different stage.

Years of teaching and medical service had placed her among the senior figures within her institution. Students who had once sat in her lectures now returned as colleagues, occupying positions within hospitals and universities across the country.

The cycle of mentorship had completed one of its natural rotations.

Teachers become elders.

Institutions continue functioning as individuals move through them.

From the vantage of the witness, this transition revealed another pattern within human societies.

Roles change.

Influence persists.

A life dedicated to service leaves traces not only within personal relationships but within the systems that continue operating long after the individual withdraws from daily activity.

In Sangli, Sarla and Naveen's clinic had become an established part of the community.

Patients arrived not only for treatment but for reassurance that familiar doctors remained present within a rapidly changing world.

The practice of medicine carries a quiet continuity.

Generations of physicians inherit knowledge refined through centuries of observation and experience.

Each doctor contributes small adjustments to that collective understanding before passing the responsibility forward.

Adi entered adulthood during these years.

Education carried her beyond the boundaries of childhood environments.

Universities introduced new questions, new disciplines, new relationships.

The pattern remained consistent.

Curiosity propagated.

Intellectual inheritance continued expressing itself through the next generation.

Meanwhile the world surrounding these individual lives continued transforming at accelerating speed.

Digital technologies reorganized communication across societies.

Information traveled instantly across distances that once required weeks or months to traverse.

Human attention began distributing itself across networks that blurred the boundaries between physical and virtual environments.

From within human perception these developments often created a sense of fragmentation.

The pace of change exceeded the rhythms through which earlier generations had organized their lives.

Yet from the perspective of awareness of the witness, these transformations represented another phase in the evolution of collective consciousness.

Human societies had always developed tools to extend perception.

Language extended memory.

Writing extended communication across time.

Printing extended knowledge across populations.

Digital networks extended awareness across the entire planet.

Each stage increased the scale at which human minds could interact with one another.

And within that expanding network, patterns of thought moved with increasing speed.

Karan occasionally encountered these developments with both fascination and caution.

The same technologies capable of accelerating discovery could also amplify confusion.

Information alone does not create understanding.

Understanding requires reflection.

Reflection requires stillness.

These realizations sometimes arrived during quiet moments—a walk beside water, a pause between meetings, an evening when the noise of daily responsibilities temporarily receded.

During such moments the mind returned once more to earlier questions.

Questions about time.

Questions about awareness.

Questions about whether the structures through which humans organize experience reflect the deeper nature of reality or merely the limitations of perception.

From the wide awareness of the witness, these reflections represented the gradual reemergence of a deeper continuity.

Ideas introduced decades earlier had not disappeared.

They had simply moved quietly beneath the surface of daily activity, waiting for moments when the mind again became receptive to them.

The witness observed these developments without attachment.

Human lives moved through phases of expansion and contraction.

Periods of intense activity alternated with moments of introspection.

Through these cycles individuals gradually refined their understanding of themselves and the systems within which they lived.

And slowly another convergence became visible.

The questions that had once shaped one life were beginning to reappear within another.

Not as direct repetition.

As a continuation.

Human consciousness rarely inherits answers.

It inherits questions.

Questions travel across generations because they remain unresolved.

Each generation examines them using the tools and experiences available within its own time.

From the wider field of awareness of the witness, this process resembled a long conversation extending across centuries.

Individuals enter the conversation briefly.

They contribute their observations.

Then they depart, leaving others to continue exploring the same mysteries.

The life once called Sharan had participated in that conversation.

Now the questions continued moving through other minds.

The witness observed these currents gradually drawing toward a deeper realization.

The separation humans perceive between observer and system is temporary.

Awareness observing the universe is itself part of the universe observing its own structure. The observed and the observer are one and the same.

The distinction between individual consciousness and universal consciousness exists primarily within the boundaries created by the limits of human perception.

Beyond those boundaries the system becomes continuous.

Observer.

Observed.

Observation.

Three aspects of the same unfolding reality.

And within that continuity the witness began recognizing something that had been present from the beginning.

There had never truly been a separation.

Only different vantage points within the same field of awareness through which existence continues discovering itself.

EPILOGUE

Continuity

Every life is a brief vantage point from which the universe examines itself.

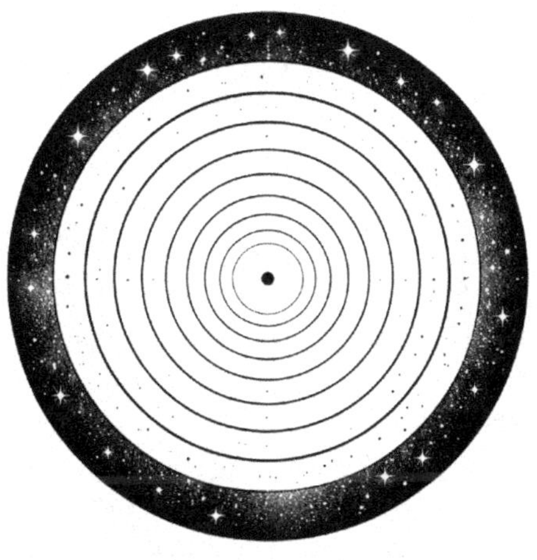

Human lives often appear complete only when viewed from a distance.

Within experience, events rarely form clear conclusions. One moment flows into the next. Decisions generate consequences that unfold long after the original intention has been forgotten.

From the vantage of awareness, the idea of an ending reveals itself as a useful fiction.

Forms begin.

Forms dissolve.

But the patterns that gave rise to them continue moving through the larger system.

The life once called Sharan had appeared within a particular time, a particular place, among a particular group of people whose lives intersected with his for a brief portion of their journeys.

That form had now dissolved.

The body returned to the elements from which it had been assembled.

The voice that once spoke through it had fallen silent.

Yet the patterns it helped shape remained active.

Ideas once spoken continued moving quietly through conversations between students and teachers.

Questions once asked continued resurfacing within minds that had never encountered the person who first raised them.

Moments of kindness offered casually years earlier continued influencing decisions made far away from their origin.

From the perspective of awareness, influence rarely travels in straight lines.

It spreads through networks of relationship, memory, and curiosity.

The smallest gesture may propagate further than the most carefully planned achievement.

The family whose lives had once gathered around that single presence continued their journeys.

Karan continued asking questions about the nature of systems and the structures underlying the material world.

Diana continued building knowledge alongside him, their partnership grounded in the quiet equilibrium that had first emerged beside the waters of Lake Mendota.

Sunita continued guiding generations of medical students whose work would touch the lives of thousands of patients they would never meet personally.

Sarla and Naveen continued serving their community in Sangli, where the rhythms of medicine and family life unfolded side by side.

Adi entered adulthood carrying forward curiosity that had begun as simple drawings beneath a child's sun.

From within human perception these lives appeared separate.

From within the wider field of awareness of the witness, they formed part of the same unfolding pattern.

Each mind influenced others.

Each action altered trajectories that extended far beyond the moment in which they occurred.

The universe does not progress through isolated events.

It evolves through relationships.

The questions that move through human consciousness form one such relationship.

They pass from generation to generation, reshaped by new experiences yet always pointing toward the same fundamental mystery.

What is the nature of existence?

What is the relationship between the observer and the observed?

Why does awareness arise within a universe capable of contemplating itself?

Human traditions have approached these questions from many directions.

Science examines the structure of matter and energy.

Philosophy analyzes the foundations of knowledge and perception.

Spiritual traditions explore the nature of consciousness beyond the boundaries of individual identity.

Each path illuminates a different aspect of the same reality.

These explorations appear not as competing explanations but as complementary attempts to understand a system far larger than any single perspective.

The witness that once observed life through the form called Sharan now recognized something that had always been present.

Awareness was never confined to one life.

It had simply been focused there temporarily.

Human experience provides a vantage point from which the universe observes itself.

When that vantage dissolves, awareness does not disappear.

It expands.

The boundaries that once defined identity dissolve into the larger field from which they originally emerged.

In that field, distinctions between observer and observed gradually lose their meaning.

The universe becomes both the question and the one asking it.

Both the pattern and the awareness recognizing the pattern.

The lives that continue unfolding within time remain expressions of that same process.

Each generation enters the world carrying questions it did not originate.

Each generation leaves the world having altered those questions slightly.

And through that continuous refinement, the universe slowly learns about itself.

From the perspective of awareness, this process has no final conclusion.

There is no ultimate answer waiting at the end of time.

There is only continued exploration.

The unfolding of existence examining its own nature through countless temporary forms.

Human beings often search for permanence.

Yet the deeper continuity lies not in preserving individual forms but in sustaining the process through which awareness continues discovering itself.

The life once called Sharan had participated in that process.

Now other lives continued the exploration.

The witness remained present within the wider field of awareness, observing without separation the unfolding patterns of existence.

And within that observation a quiet understanding settled with perfect clarity.

Nothing had truly ended.

The journey had simply changed its perspective.

The vantage changes.

The awareness that witnessed it does not.

Author

Chetan (Chet) Rao, Ph.D., is a scientist, entrepreneur, and writer whose work explores the deeper patterns underlying human experience. His writing moves between narrative, reflection, and philosophical inquiry, drawing on both the analytical traditions of modern science and the contemplative insights of older spiritual traditions.

Born and raised in India, Rao studied engineering at the Indian Institute of Technology, Bombay, before continuing his graduate work in the United States. His professional life has spanned research, technology, and global advisory work, where questions about systems, complexity, and human decision-making often intersect.

Alongside these pursuits, he has maintained a lifelong interest in the nature of consciousness and the ways human beings seek meaning within the structures of ordinary life.

The Weight of Nothing: Reflections from Above is the concluding volume of **The Weight Trilogy**, which includes *The Weight of Shadows: Reflections from the Edge* and *The Weight of Grace: Reflections from the Center*. Together the three books explore the movement of a life through struggle, balance, and the deeper awareness that emerges when the boundaries of individual identity begin to dissolve.

www.ingramcontent.com/pod-product-compliance
Lightning Source LLC
LaVergne TN
LVHW010947110826
845149LV00015B/3246

9798993691190